Rev. J. Warren Smouse.

THE HISTORY

OF THE

Smouse Family

OF AMERICA

BY J. WARREN SMOUSE

MARTINSBURG, PA., 1908

HERALD Print, Martinsburg, Pa

WINDHAM PRESS
CLASSIC REPRINTS

INTRODUCTION.

Mr. Emerson says, "No man is worth his room in the world who is not commanded by a legitimate object of thought." Again he says, "The few superior persons in each community are so by their steadiness to reality and their neglect of appearances." What he says of persons in both statements may with equal propriety be said of books.

The author who is "commanded by a legitimate object of thought," has the first requisite necessary to make a book "worth its room in the world," and if he writes a book animated by "its steadiness to reality and neglect of appearances," it ought to have a place in the world.

Books like people have various ways of getting into their places in the world. This book comes and seeks its place by force of circumstances which could not well be resisted. The circumstances need not be enumerated. But the chief circumstance, or primary object was to give an historical and biographical sketch of the family in America.

It may seem selfish to mention the amount of labor that has been necessary in the accumulation of so much data, and this seems the proper place to express how much the author is indebted to George Smouse, Elmer S. Burket and John M. Smouse, members of the Committee on Data, and also the Rev. J. M. S. Isenberg, B. D., for the facts, and in many instances the very language herein given. But in a multitude of instances the facts refused to appear in suitable and concise form, and so had to be fashioned and rewritten.

It would have been a comparatively easy task to have inventoried all the facts. But that would not have been a noteworthy labor. There has not been another such ransacking of libraries, archives and church records in recent years, and although much has been obtained and accomplished by this diligent research, the author had to sift and analyze traditions and discover facts in many instances, and feels assured that the truth has been arrived at.

In the list of descendants it has been impossible to have all the names given and all the dates exact, and in this respect we must ask indulgence.

The honored and respected record of our ancestors should stimulate each and all of us to make the future name of the family still more honored and respected, and thereby transmit a legacy to our posterity of which they may be proud, and by so doing inspire them to attain unto the highest niche in the temple of honor and fame, thus amply rewarding us for all our labor and toil.

J. WARREN SMOUSE.

Martinsburg. Pa., 1908.

THE FIRST REUNION.

About one-eighth of a mile north-east of the Pennsylvania Railroad depot in the famous mining village of Henrietta, Pa., stood a log house one and one-half stories high, surrounded by a beautiful orchard of a variety of choice fruit, and just south of the road leading to the Tussey Mountain, whose lofty heights towering thousands of feet above, only a short distance east. Here lived Michael and Dorothy (Loose) Smouse, the greater part of their lives, or from 1838 to the time of their death, the former in 1875 and the latter in 1891.

During the summer of 1895, F. S. Burket, a grandson of Michael and Dorothy Smouse, and Administrator of the estate of Dorothy Smouse, deceased, sold the above-named property to John L. Smouse, a son of Michael and Dorothy Smouse. Two years later, or in 1897, the above John L. Smouse sold the property to Harry Ketner. Thus after fifty-nine (59) years of ownership by this one family of Smouses, the property went into other hands, and at the confirmation of this sale the thought came into the minds of Mrs. Elias Burket and Mrs. M. B. Stonerook, daughters of Michael and Dorothy Smouse, to hold a family reunion on the old homestead, before possession would be given to the new owners. In view thereof E. S. Burket, a grandson of the old owners, called a meeting for the last Saturday in October, 1897, inviting all the children, grandchildren and great-grandchildren of

Michael and Dorothy Smouse, to enjoy a day together.

The following children with their wives and husbands were present:

David F. Smouse and wife Lizzie.

John L. Smouse and wife Lizzie.

Elizabeth (Smouse) Burket and husband Elias.

Barbary (Smouse) Coy and husband John.

Nancy (Smouse) Stonerook and husband M. B.

Maggie (Smouse) Stewart and husband John.

Grand Children.

Elmer S. Burket and wife Annie.

Mrs. Annie Stoner.

Sadie Houp and husband William.

Lizzie Shultz and husband Porter.

Mrs. Laura Hartman.

Miss Dora Burket, Miss Ella Burket.

Miss Rosa Smouse, Miss Nellie Smouse.

Miss Dora Stewart, Eddie Stewart, Robert Stewart.

Henry Stewart, David Stewart, Freddie Smouse.

James Stonerook, Charles Stonerook and Mearl Coy.

Great Grand Children.

Roy Burket, Clark Burket, Rebecca Burket, Don. B. Shultz, John Stoner, Lloyd Stoner, Blair Hartman, Mary Hartman, Ruth Hartman and Wesley Houp.

The youngest son of Michael and Dorothy Smouse was not present, he living in Johnstown, Pa., and the invitation to attend said reunion failed to reach him in time.

The second reunion was held the first Saturday in September, 1898, at which time the family of Michael and Dorothy Smouse were fully represented and an enjoyable day was spent in reminiscences, games, &c.

In the following year, viz. 1899, the Rev. J. W. Smouse succeeded in having members of several Smouse families to

meet with the Michael and Dorothy Smouse family, and
prominent among the number assembled on that festive day
was George Smouse, Sr., of Bedford, Pa. From his knowledge
of the Smouses in America, the writer of this book received
valuable data, as well as great encouragement. It was at
this gathering that the Smouse Association of America was
formed. Its object was to gather data, and to endeavor to
bring all the different families to participate in the next reunion, to be held the following year, at Ashcom, Pa., on the
farm once owned and occupied by John Smouse. The officers chosen were F. S. Burket, Altoona, Pa., President; J. W.
Smouse, Yellow Creek, Pa., Secretary; A. M. Smouse, Martinsburg, Pa., Treasurer. A data committee was also selected at that time, to co-operate with the officers of the Association. The members of said committee were: Geo. Smouse,
Bedford, Pa.; John M. Smouse, Henrietta, Pa.; and Elmer S.
Burket, Altoona, Pa.

The inspiration of that day had such a marvelous effect
that the annual reunions since then bring together thousands
of kith and kin from the Atlantic to the Pacific and from the
lakes to the gulf.

The eleventh reunion of the Association held at Saxton,
Pa., August 29, 1907, selected the following named persons
as a committee on publication: J. W. Smouse, Thomas F.
Smouse, George Smouse, Win Smouse, E. S. Feight, E. S.
Burket, B. F. Gibbony, John Koontz and S. S. Nicodemus.

J. W. Smouse was unanimously selected to prepare the
manuscript for the publishing of this book, and E. S. Burket
was selected as Secretary-Treasurer of said committee and
also soliciting agent.

The Name and Family.

The family is of German descent or extraction, and the
language of the Fatherland gave place to the English, more

than a generation ago among the Smouses of America. Prior
to 1810, the name was written Schmaus, excepting in a few
instances, it was spelled Smouse as early as 1790. In Germany it is still written Schmaus, with the exception of those
families who live in Alsace, who spell the name Von Schmau-
sen, yet they are descendants of Carl Smouse, born June 11,
1281. Many of the present generation are doubtless ignor-
ant of the significance of the name. At the time of the great
migrations, A. D., 500, and the division of Germany, all
names of German origin were given or assumed by families,
and referred to character, location, position or rank. The
name Schmaus means robust, hearty and retund, and it also
signifies loyalty.

In the province of Saxe-Coberg the name appears in
history for the first time, and it was in the years 679-685 that
Carl Schmaus was stationed at the town of Wohlsdorf as
Colonel of "The Life Guards." In the year 715 we find that
John Schmaus located at Coblentz and practiced medicine and
surgery. He was also prominent in the affairs of state. His
son, Peter Schmaus, was also a noted physician and surgeon.
Albrecht Schmaus was a Captain in the German artillery service
during the years 1768-1779. Many of the Schmauses in Germany and the Netherlands are prominent in the affairs of
state. John Jacob Schmaus was a member of the Reichstad
when he died 1892. John Henry Schmaus of Leipsic, is rec-
ognized as one of the ablest surgeons in the Kingdom.

The family in America has been, and still is noted for
industry, progress and patriotism. From the time of, and
during the French and Indian war, to the present time, some
of those who bear the name have been in the armies of
America.

In the field of Merchandise we find a vast number who
are successful and prosperous. Many are famous, but the
name occurs frequently among those who are teachers, doc-

tors, lawyers and ministers; in most of the callings of life representatives of the family are to be found, reflecting honor and credit on their chosen calling.

As the families intermarried with those of other religious faiths, (the Lutheran church being the church of their fathers), or as they located in communities where the church of their faith was not, and being a people who loved their Lord and Master more than their denomination, they identified themselves with the church most convenient. Thus we find the name on the rolls of Presbyterian, Lutheran, Baptist, United Brethren, Methodist Episcopal, Brethren and other churches. Intelligence and industry have marked them, and as a result the family has been well represented in prominent positions in the church.

With the changes of location and church relation, there have been changes in political faith. Before the Civil War the family was solidly Democratic, and many are so yet. But we find many of the family to-day who are Republicans, some who are Prohibitionists, and some who are Populists.

The author of this book has been enabled through church records to trace the family lineage back to 1281, not a link being missed in the chain. Charles (Schmaus) Smouse was born June 11, 1281, and he was a merchant in his native city. His descendants were prominent in mechanism, medicine, merchandizing and theology. His son Jacob was born April 28, 1319, who was the father of nine children. His son Adam was born April 23, 1342. Adam was married at the age of 20 years, and was the father of ten children. His son Daniel was born September 19, 1370. Daniel had but two children, a son and daughter. His son Peter was born July 14, 1401. Peter was the father of six girls and four boys. Henry, his son, was born June 8, 1436. Henry had but one child, a son, whom he named Michael. This son was born February 12, 1460. Michael was the father of eight children, all boys.

His first-born he named Henry, who was born November 20, 1485. Henry was the father of Charles, who was born October 20, 1521, and at the age of 28 years married Mary Beacker, and had but one child when he (Henry) died. This child was John Schmaus, born March 19, 1550. John was the father of Adam, who was born January 24, 1583. Adam married Gretchen (Margaret) Bauer, and had six children born unto them. His son William was born December 14, 1610. He was married to Elizabeth Stuker and had seven children. George, his son, was born May 19, 1638, and was married to Anna Pflug. He was the father of eight children. His son Peter, was born August 23, 1655. Peter Schmaus was united in marriage to Mary Fleishman. To this union were born six children. Henry, the first son, was born February 2, 1688. Henry was married to Catherine Foltz and had nine children—Henry, John, Anna, Mary, Pheba, James, Peter, David and Elizabeth.

John Smouse, son of Henry, and grandson of Peter Smouse, was born April 5, 1721. He in company with Casper Latz, Valentine Wilt, Elias Nicholas Bender, Philip Sneltzer and Christian Miller, set sail at Bremen for the New World as it was then called, and after a tempestuous voyage landed at Baltimore, Maryland, September 19, 1738.

He remained in the city of Baltimore for only a few weeks, when he went to Loudon county, Virginia. He engaged with an old pioneer to drive team, which vocation he followed until the Spring of 1740, when he began farming. He also had a team of his own carrying freight from Baltimore into the settlements in Loudoun county, Virginia. During the French and Indian war he and Christian Miller were in the employ of the Government. They were hauling supplies and helped to cut a road from Carlisle to Fort Bedford. He was present with his team when that fierce battle was fought at Bloody Run, now Everett. He was one of eighteen men who with Captain Stone rescued six prisoners that were to be burned by the Indians. On the day following that of the battle Captain Stone being apprised of the doom awaiting the captives, called for volunteers to go at dead of night and rescue, if possible, their unfortunate comrades. Eighteen responded, and at midnight they started. Silently they marched through the forest, and when the first rosy hue of dawn appeared on the eastern horizon, with brave hearts and strong hands they dashed among the wigwams of the Indian camp and rescued their comrades, only one of the eighteen having received a slight wound.

It was at this time that he first saw the land or piece of ground in Bedford county, Pennsylvania, which he purchased in 1785. The deed for said land being dated August 24, 1785.

He was united in marriage to Mary Wohlfrom, of Loudoun county, Virginia. She was a redemptionist, that is, she had to serve four years as servant girl to a wealthy land owner, who had paid her fare, or passage from Germany to America. At the expiration of the tenure of service she had redeemed her pledge and was free. To the union of those two hearts were born nine children—Peter, George Adam, John, David, Michael, Charles, Catharine, Susan and Matilda. In the fall of 1785 he moved from Loudoun county, Virginia, and settled with his family on the farm now known as the Ashcom farm, Bedford county, Pennsylvania. His sons, Peter and George Adam, were soldiers from Loudoun county, Virginia, in the Revolutionary War. They were present at Yorktown when Cornwallis surrendered.

In 1791 Peter Smouse settled near Cumberland, Maryland. He was married to a Miss Heckman. He was the father of seven children— Henry, David, Daniel, Peter, John, George and Maria.

Henry Smouse married Catherine Rice and was the

father of eleven children—George, born June 12, 1804; Sophia, born March 6, 1806; Julia Ann, born January 22, 1810; Elizabeth, born June 22, 1813; Elemarie, born October 12, 1815; Henry Peter, born September 2, 1817; John Jacob, born November 20, 1819; Henry Daniel, born January 10, 1822; Priscilla, born June 17, 1824; Henry, born September 2, 1826; David, born June 2, 1828.

Henry Peter Smouse was married to Elizabeth Neff, June 2, 1844. She is still living near Cumberland, Maryland. She is the mother of the following named children: Harriet Ann, born 1845; John Neff, born November 25, 1846, (He is in Pittsburg, Pennsylvania); Emma V., born August 25, 1848, married to A. A. Wilson, of Cumberland, Maryland; Laura, born August 31, 1850; Theodore B. born September 9, 1852; Charles A., born October 31, 1856; Mary E., born September 11, 1854; William H., born December 6, 1858; Gussie E., born July 2, 1861; Smelda May, born December 23, 1863; Sallie W., born July 29, 1866; Peter Bender, born June 14, 1869.

Sophia Smouse, daughter of Peter Smouse, was married to Daniel Folk. They located in the State of Missouri, where they died. No record of their family could be obtained.

Julia Ann Smouse, daughter of Peter Smouse, was united in marriage to William Frantz. Her children are: Joseph, Daniel, John, William, Charles, and two daughters, Mrs. L. Gurley and Mrs. H. S. Brotemarkle.

Joseph, son of William and Julia Ann Frantz, was married to Rosanna Smith. To this union were born these children: Lloyd, John N., Henry O., Patrick H. H., Richard S. Mc. H., Sarah and Mary J.

Sarah, daughter of Joseph and Rosanna Frantz, was united in marriage to Thomas J. Slifer, September 5, 1872. To this union were born these children: Edith E., born November 4, 1873, married Charles W. McIntosh October 25, 1899; Alva G., born June 7, 1875, married Clara Pflug September 18, 1904; Walter J., born April 11, 1876; William T., born July 28, 1877, married Ethel Shore October 10, 1900; Lillian M., born May 18, 1879; Bessie M. born November 2, 1880; Oscar M., born November 22, 1881; John E., born February 23, 1884, and Garnett, born July 27, 1887.

Mary J., daughter of Joseph and granddaughter of Julia Ann (Smouse) Frantz, was united in marriage to Harvey Wilson A. D., 1875. To this union were born these children: Frank, Rose, George, Blanche, Ernest and Edna.

Frank, son of Mary J. and Harvey Wilson, was born June 11, 1876. In 1898, he was married to Cora Keyser. One child was born to them - Ruth Wilson, born 1900.

George, son of Harvey and Mary J. Wilson, was born 1880. He is married to Myrtle Wentling. To them two sons were born - Alvin, born in 1901, and Harvey, born in 1902.

Rose, Blanche, Ernest and Edna Wilson are still single.

William F., son of William and Julia Ann (Smouse) Frantz, was united in marriage to Eliza M————. To this union were born Robert L., September 12, 1876. Helen C., December 23, 1878. Julia J., March 4, 1881. Ralph W., July 9, 1885. Guy J., Dec. 8, 1887. D. Raymond, May 27, 1891, and Edith May, May 6, 1893.

Charles W., son of William and Julia Ann (Smouse) Frantz, was united in marriage to Annie L. Burket January 9, 1882. To this union were born the following children: Daisy Victory, Charles Walter, Gracie, James Howard, Irvin Shannon, Gussie Lee, Lottie Blanche, Anna Lula May, Daniel Author, Mary Alice Ruth, Carrie Pearl, Clarence Roderick; Oscar Benjamin Nicholas, Roy Lewis Edgar, Herman Brace, Lillian Edith, and Helen Sarah. Daisy Victory married Mr. Reggie Twigg, and Charles Walter married Miss Nellie Brotemarkle.

Grandchildren of C. W. and Annie Frantz — Eldon Oliver Shields Paxton, Charles Edward Twigg.

Elizabeth Smouse, daughter of Henry and granddaughter of Peter Smouse, was born June 20, 1813, died February 21, 1872. She was married to John James of Rainsburg, Pa. To this union were born four sons and three daughters—John, William, Henry, Rachael, Mary, Maria and David.

John, son of Elizabeth (Smouse) James, was born August 17, 1842. He was united in marriage to Catharine Walters January 28, 1869. He is a farmer at Beegleton, Pa. His children are: Plummer, born February 13, 1872. Bertie, born June 2, 1870. Bruce, born October 27, 1876, and June, October 7, 1879.

William, son of Elizabeth (Smouse) James, is a farmer at Charlesville, Pa. He was born April 12, 1840. Married Mattie Beegle January 27, 1870. His children are: Herbert, born May 2, 1871. Ralph, born April 10, 1878.

Henry, son of Elizabeth (Smouse) James, is a merchant at Bedford, Pa. He was born October 5, 1844. He was united in marriage to Sophia E. Shaffer January 27, 1870. His children are: Mary R., born November 1, 1870. Fannie F., born April 12, 1873. Frank H., born August 26, 1877. Charles, born August 26, 1877, died in infancy. Harry Clay, born September 7, 1881. Bessie E., born November 24, 1884. Edwin, born October 14, 1887.

Rachael, daughter of Elizabeth (Smouse) James, was born May 1, 1838. She married ———— Ake, of Findlay, Ohio. Her offspring are: Clara, born in 1860. Emma, born March 2, 1862. Jennie, born August 9, 1864. Sadie, born May 15, 1866. Minnie, born April 9, 1868, and Frank, born March 14, 1869.

Mary, daughter of Elizabeth (Smouse) James was born June 2, 1834. She married Jacob Barnhart, of Bedford, Pa. Her children are: John C., William C., Orrie D., Harry C., and Emma. Mrs. Barnhart died July 29, 1903.

Maria, daughter of Elizabeth (Smouse) James, was born

June 22, 1836. She married ——— Amick, and had these children: Stanly, Maud, Margaret and John.

David, son of Elizabeth (Smouse) James, was born December 18, 1846. He is single and is a farmer.

Plummer James, son of John, is a farmer at Beegleton, Pa. He is married to Ella M. Diehl.

Bertie, son of John James, is single.

Bruce James is a machinist at Newark, Ohio. He married Miss Florence Early February 22, 1901.

June James, married Samuel Beegle, of Newark, Ohio, April 10, 1900. Issue, Plummer and Raymond.

Herbert, son of William and Mattie James, was born May 2, 1870. He is a farmer, and is still single.

Ralph, son of William and Mattie James, was born April 10, 1878. He was united in marriage to Bertha Diehl September 15, 1901. He is a farmer at Beegleton, Pa.

Mary, daughter of Henry and Sophia James, was born November 1, 1870. She was joined in wedlock to John C. Roberts, of Bedford, Pa., June 2, 1898. One son was born to this union. Lamont J., born June 20, 1901.

Fannie F. James, milliner, Bedford, Pa.

Frank H. James, dentist, Bedford, Pa.

Harry C. James, lawyer, Bedford, Pa.

Bessie E. James, teacher, Bedford, Pa., and Edwin James, clerk, Bedford, Pa., are children of Henry and Sophia James.

Clara, daughter of Rachael (James) Ake, married Albert James, of Rainsburg, Pa. To them were born two children.

Emma, Jennie, Sadie, Minnie and Frank Ake are all at home at Findlay, Ohio.

John C. Barnhart is clerking in Pittsburg, Pa. He is married to Myra Keyser.

William Barnhart, a carpenter, at Bedford, Pa. He married Anna Dickens. Issue, Jacob and Emory.

Orrie Barnhart married Jennie Pell, of Spear Fish, South

Dakota, where he is engaged at carpentering. Two girls were born to this union—Mary and Lula.

Harry Barnhart married Bessie Moor, of New York city, where he is employed as a salesman.

Emma Barnhart married E. W. Woodruff, of Washington, D. C. She has two children—Edward and Lena.

Stanley Amick married May Fetter, of Altoona, Pa., where they reside.

Maude Amick married Mr. Young, of Hollidaysburg, Pa.

Margaret Amick married Harry Hall, of Hollidaysburg, Pa.

John Amick is single and lives at St. Clairsville, Pa.

Ela Marie Smouse married James Russell. They moved from Maryland to Missouri in 1847, then on to Texas in 1852. Mr. Russell died in 1862, and Mrs. E. M. Russell died in McClellan county, Texas, in 1886.

Their children, five boys and four girls, were Cathrine, Martha, Henry, Elnathan, James R., Eva, Maria, Abraham W., Lula and Charles, of which only three are living. Martha Russell married W. W. Glasgow, of West, Texas, in 1869, had five children, two living. W. R. Glasgow, West, Texas; Katie Glasgow Holt, Amarillo, Texas.

Lizzie Glasgow married S. A. McClellan. She died in 1881, leaving two children, Crockett McClellan, West, Texas; and Len McClellan, Amarillo, Texas.

W. R. Glasgow, born in 1885, married in 1900, has two children—Wilma, born in 1902, died in 1903; and Mima L. Glasgow, born in 1904.

Katie Glasgow, married in 1887, has three children—Merle, born in 1888; Willie Joe, born in 1890; and Enida Eva, born 1893.

Crockett McClellan, grandson of W. W. and Martha Russell Glasgow, married May Johnson in 1898, has one son, Cecil McClellan, born 1890.

A. W. Russell married Emma Westmoreland. Has four children—Allie Russell, married Mr. Shaw, and died in 1891. James Russell, Weatherford, Oklahoma; Colonel A. Russell, West, Texas, and Daniel Russell, West, Texas.

Lula Russell married W. H. Westmoreland. She died May 26, 1903, aged 49 years. She was the mother of eight children—Edgar Westmoreland, of Abbott, Texas.

Gertrude Westmoreland married S. T. Christian, West, Texas. Has three children—Roy, Shirley and Robert.

Russell Westmoreland, of West, Texas.

Josh Westmoreland, of West, Texas.

May Westmoreland died in 1896.

Hattie Westmoreland, West, Texas.

Sterling Westmoreland, West, Texas.

Ida Westmoreland died in 1890.

Cathrine Russell married T. Tinsley, after whose death she married D. C. Carr. She had nine children—James Tinsley, Abbott, Texas; Win Tinsley, Abbott, Texas; J. D. Tinsley, Abbott, Texas, died in 1904; Bettie Carr Ellis, Abbott, Texas; Mollie Carr Jones, Hillsboro, Texas; Mattie Carr Aplin, Hillsboro, Texas; Minnie Carr Hooker, deceased; Laura Carr Hooker, Abbott, Texas, and Dee Carr, deceased.

Cathrine Russell Carr died in 1885.

Eva Maria Russell, West Plains, Missouri.

Elnathan Russell, deceased, married Mollie Westmoreland, had two children.

Lula Russell, deceased; Jessie Russell married F. Thomas, Waco, Texas; Charles Russell married Meetie Adams, died leaving five children—Ella, Oscar, George, Bessie and Hattie Russell.

John Jacob Smouse was born November 20, 1819, near Cumberland, Allegheny county, Maryland. He was united in marriage with Sarah E. James, of Bedford, Pennsylvania, in the spring of 1850. They had seven children—George W.

J., David W., Lessing Eugene, John Reese, Thomas Lee, Carrie V., and Clara Gladys (Smouse).

John Jacob Smouse lived all his life in Allegheny county, Maryland, with the exception of two years spent in Missouri when a young man. He followed farming, or managed the farm. But being of a mechanical turn of mind, directed his attention to contracting, building a large number of bridges, school houses, churches, mills and other buildings, many of which are standing at the present time.

His chief delight was to work with machinery of all kinds, and while in feeble health was caught and killed by a belt in a mill March 25, 1885.

He was one of the prominent men in the community in which he lived, and took an active part in all public affairs, being one of the most distinguished members of the Methodist Protestant church, to which he contributed largely from his means. His wife, Sarah E. Smouse, is living, in good health, aged 79 years, spending most of her time in Chicago.

George W. J. (Smouse), born April 14, 1851, died April 10, 1871.

David W. (Smouse), born October 15, 1853, now living in Des Moines, Iowa, practicing medicine.

Lessing Eugene (Smouse), born February 24, 1856, now living in Glenwood, Iowa; has been an invalid all his life following an attack of spinal meningitis.

John Reese (Smouse), born October 27, 1858, lived in Cumberland, Maryland, until the past year; moved to Iowa.

Thomas Lee (Smouse), born December 5, 1860; at the present time living at Glenwood, Iowa, on a fruit farm; married Emma Peterson January 1, 1894; they have two children, both girls.

Carrie V. (Smouse), born April 3, 1863; married James D. Wincow December, 1886, died in Cumberland, Maryland, where she had lived all her life. She left two daughters— Gladys Wincow and Carrie Wincow.

Clara Gladys (Smouse), born June 3), 1867; married to Elmer A. Todd October 19, 1887; now living in Chicago. They have no children.

Dr. D. W. Smouse.

Dr. David Wilson Smouse was born October 15, 1853, near Cumberland, Maryland, being a son of John J. and Sarah E. Smouse. He attended the country schools until fifteen years of age, when his father put him in a country store, known as ————, where he remained for two and one-half years, after which he entered the Rainsburg Seminary for two years.

He was then sent to the Maryland University of Medicine for two years, the last year of which he spent in the University hospital as interne, graduating in the Spring of 1876.

The Doctor located in Monroe, Iowa, where he remained practicing his profession until the fall of 1879, when he moved to Des Moines, Iowa, where he has remained in active practice ever since.

He now enjoys one of the largest consulting and surgical practices in the state of Iowa.

He is chief medical director of the Central Life Assurance Society of the United States of America, as well as of the Bankers' Accident Insurance Company, both of Des Moines, Iowa.

The Doctor is Vice President of one bank and on the directory board of two others, as well as holding other positions of trust.

He was married in 1881 in Waterloo, Iowa, to Amanda H. Cummins. They have no children.

Henry Daniel, son of Henry, (who died in December, 1849) and grandson of Peter, and great grandson of John Smouse, (who came to this country from Hesse-Darmstad,

Germany, on the ship "Thistle," which qualified at Baltimore, Maryland, September 19, 1738.) His father, Henry Smouse, had one brother, Daniel, and one sister, who married —————— Chapman. His grandfather, Peter Smouse, had five brothers, George Adam, John, David, Michael and Charles, and three sisters, who by marriage became Cathrine Ritchey, Susan Koontz and Matilda Koontz. These two sisters married brothers whose descendants are still in Bedford county, Pa.

Henry Daniel Smouse was born five miles north-east of Cumberland, on the Bedford road, January 10, 1822, at the brick house farm owned by his father and mother, Henry and Cathrine Smouse, which farm was bought in the year 1800 by Peter Smouse, and by him sold to Henry Smouse in 1832, and by him sold to Henry Daniel in 1843. He had four brothers, Peter, John J., David and Henry. Five sisters, Julia Ann, Sophia, Maria, Priscilla and Elizabeth.

Henry Daniel was married twice, first to Anna Brotemarkle June 6, 1843; she died April 14, 1844. On December 5, 1845, he was married to Elizabeth Brotemarkle, sister of his first wife, (who were daughters of Henry Brotemarkle, a prominent citizen and large land owner, who lived in Little Valley, four miles north of Cumberland, who was a son of Christopher Brotemarkle, who came from Germany.) Elizabeth was born June 14, 1824.

Henry Daniel Smouse lived on his farm of nearly six hundred acres until April, 1867, during which time he was a prominent, prosperous and highly respected citizen of the community. He was Superintendent of the Sabbath school for many years, and was also one of the leading officers in Zion Lutheran church, which was built on his farm, the land for the church house and cemetery being donated by him.

Henry Daniel Smouse had by his first marriage one son, John Henry, and by his second marriage four sons, Leonard, Winfield Arnold and Newton, who died when about two

years old, and four daughters, Amanda, who married George
L. Conard; Mary Virginia, who married Frederick N. Ander-
son; Sarah Elnora, who married Seneca B. Dewey; Rosa Van
Lear, who married Charles W. Stephens.

In April 1867, having sold his farm to Daniel Long, he
moved with all his family except John Henry, to Washington, Iowa, where he bought a home and business property
and engaged in the bakery business with his sons Leonard and
Winfield, retiring from active business in 1883. In politics
he was a Republican. There being no Lutheran church at
Washington he and most of his family united with the First
Presbyterian church of Washington, to which he was soon
after elected a ruling elder, which office he efficiently filled
until his death, which occurred April 28, 1899.

He was buried in Elmwood cemetery, Washington, Iowa.
He was very active in promoting temperance and in favor of
prohibition and lived a very consistent Christian life. His
wife, Elizabeth, now lives at Washington, Iowa. She is 82
years of age.

John Henry (Smouse), son of Henry Daniel Smouse, was
born five miles north of Cumberland, March 31, 1844. He
was married to Ella Barnhart, to whom were born three children—Viola May, who died at Washington, Iowa, May 17,
1884, Harry Ulysses and Clifford.

John Henry Smouse lived at Cumberland, Maryland,
working at the tanner's trade until 1874, when he moved to
Washington, Iowa, where he engaged in different kinds of
business until 1883, when he moved to San Francisco, California, where he now resides.

Leonard Smouse, son of Henry Daniel, was born on the
old farm five miles north-east of Cumberland, Maryland, November 11, 1846, where he lived until he was twenty years
old. He was educated at Cumberland Academy, Rainsburg
Seminary, and Duff College, Pittsburg. He taught several

terms of school near Flintstone, Maryland. In 1867 he went to Washington, Iowa, clerked until 1870, and then associated himself with his father and brother, Winfield, in the grocery and bakery business until 1872, when they engaged in the hardware and implement business until 1883, in which business they were very successful. He invested in valuable real estate, to which interest he has devoted his time since.

He was married to Elizabeth Ellen Kilgore November 7, 1871, to whom were born two daughters— Ethel, who married Frank Hasting Wells, and Edith, who married John Michael Bowman. His wife died October 23, 1884. He was married to Alice Amelia Smith June 11, 1885. No issue to last marriage. In politics he is a Republican.

For over twenty-five years he has been a member of the First Presbyterian church, which he has served for many years as trustee. His home and residence is in Washington, Iowa.

Winfield Smouse, better known as Win Smouse, is a son of Henry Daniel Smouse, grandson of Henry Smouse, great grandson of Peter Smouse, great great grandson of John Smouse, the progenitor of the Smouse family in America.

Win Smouse was born on the old homestead farm (the brick house farm), five miles north-east of Cumberland, Maryland, January 17, 1849. He was educated at the Cumberland Academy and Rainsburg Seminary, and taught one term of school at the Union school house, near Smouse's Mill; he was then but 18 years old.

In April, 1867, he moved with his father's family to Washington, Iowa. On September 23, 1873, he was married to Elizabeth Smith, daughter of Hugh Smith, a merchant of Washington, Iowa. Mrs. Smouse was born in Philadelphia, Pennsylvania. They have one daughter, Jessie Belle, born July 14, 1874. She was married to Ralph Erskin Daugherty, October 25, 1899.

Win Smouse was employed by C. L. Keedy on the second day after his arrival in Washington April 1867, as a clerk in his drug store at $25 dollars per month. In the following July he was employed by Blair & Brocaw, dry goods merchants, at $35 dollars per month. The following year they advanced his salary to $500. The next year to $600 per year. Early in the spring of 1870 he left said firm and formed a partnership with his brother Leonard in the grocery and bakery business, under the firm name of L. & W. Smouse. On July, 1872, they sold out this business (in which they were very successful) and bought the largest hardware and implement business in the city, and for ten years they transacted a very large and profitable business, clearing over forty thousand dollars. In 1881 he was solicited to take a position in the First National Bank and the Washington County Savings Bank; he accepted the position of assistant cashier in the latter. At the end of one year he resigned this position and entered the real estate, exchange and loan business, besides investing in valuable real estate, the Washington Light plant, (of which he is President) and trading largely in stocks of merchandise, live stock and other property, in which he has been unusually successful, accumulating a large amount of land, town and city property, bank stocks and manufacturing interests. In 1882 he platted Win Smouse's East Side addition to Washington, 98 lots. In 1884 he platted Win Smoue's second addition to Washington of 130 lots. In 1892 he platted Highland Park addition of 430 lots. In this addition he laid out and beautified a six acre park with an artificial lake of three acres, built a boat house, &c. In 1895 he platted the Columbian addition to Washington of 296 lots. In 1898 he and his brother Leonard platted L. & W. Smouse's North-East addition of 90 lots. In 1882 he built the fine large three-story brick residence one block east of the public square, now owned by the Washington Commercial Club. In 1893 he bought the most valuable lot on the south-east corner of the public square and built the best and most modern brick block in the city, known as the Columbian Block, in which he has his residence and office.

In 1902 he platted and put on the market the new town of Haskins and spent over twenty thousand dollars in new buildings, side-walks, shade trees, etc. He has built more store buildings and houses and is the present owner of more real estate and pays more taxes than any other man in Washington.

In politics he is a Prohibition Republican. He has never been an office seeker. In 1896 he was appointed unanimously at a joint session of the Iowa State Legislature a trustee of the insane hospital at Mt. Pleasant, which office he held with credit until the trustee system was abolished by the State. In 1869 he united with the organization of Good Templars, at which time there were four breweries and about thirty saloons and drug stores selling liquor in the county. For years he was active in fighting the license of the liquor traffic in Washington. He was chairman of the County Central Committee during the campaign from 1880 to 1882, which had for its object the amending of the Constitution of the State prohibiting the manufacture and sale of intoxicating liquors as a beverage. The county was carried for prohibition by a large majority. In 1884 he was elected President of the County Temperance Alliance and director for the First District State Temperance Alliance, the object of which was to enforce the prohibitory laws, which succeeded in closing up all the breweries and saloons so that at this time and for many years past there have been no saloons nor drug stores selling liquors in Washington county. He united with the Zion Lutheran church near Cumberland, Maryland, in 1862, and on going to Washington, Iowa, he placed his church letter with the First Presbyterian church of the city, which church he served as secretary and afterwards for many years as superintendent of the Sabbath school. He served for twenty-five years as deacon and for some years past has been a ruling elder. He was chairman of the building committee that in 1892 built the fine brick church for the First Presbyterian church in Washington, Ia., contributing more than any other person. He is also a member of the board of trustees of Parsons College at Fairfield, Iowa, a Presbyterian institution.

Amanda Smouse Conard, daughter of Henry Daniel Smouse, was born January 7, 1851, five miles north-east of Cumberland, Maryland. She located in Washington, Iowa, with her father's family in April, 1867. She married George L. Conard, July 1, 1886, from whom she was divorced on account of cruelty. To them was born one son, Cecil Glenn. She is a member of the First Presbyterian church of her adopted city. She is residing with her mother, Mrs. Henry D. Smouse, at Washington, Iowa.

Arnold Smouse, son of Henry Daniel, was born April 21, 1853, on the old farm five miles north-east of Cumberland, Maryland. He went with his father's family to Iowa in 1867. He was educated in the common schools and Washington Academy. After graduating he clerked for several years, when in 1880 he bought an interest in the hardware business with his brothers Leonard and Winfield. 1883 he sold his interest in the hardware and went to Des Moines and engaged in the grocery business. He remained several years in this lucrative business in the Capital City, when he sold his store and returned to Washington and formed a partnership with C. W. Stephens in the grocery and produce business. It was while in Des Moines he met, wooed, and married Florence G. Ingersoll. After a few years in Washington he sold his interest in the grocery and produce business and moved to Mount Vernon, Iowa, and engaged in the book and stationery business. He was appointed postmaster by President Cleveland, which office he filled with credit for more than four years, or until his death, March 6, 1898. He had one child, a daughter, Florence, who with her mother, now resides in Syracuse, New York. In politics Arnold Smouse was a Democrat. He was a prominent Mason, also a Modern Woodman.

Mary Virginia, daughter of Henry Daniel Smouse, was born near Cumberland, Maryland. When but twelve years old, she left her native state with her father's family and located at Washington, Iowa. She was married to Fred N. Anderson, superintendent of the Washington Illuminating Company. They had two sons born unto them, Howard Lessing and Henry Donald. She is a member of the Presbyterian church, and a graduate of the High school, and also Washington Academy. Her present residence is at Washington, Iowa.

Sarah Eleanor, daughter of Henry Daniel Smouse, was born December 17, 1860, near Cumberland, Maryland. She was seven years of age when her family moved to Iowa. She graduated from the Washington High school and Academy. She was married to Seneca B. Dewey, a jeweler by trade. To them were born two children, Winifred, who died in infancy, and Arthur Clare. She is a member of the Presbyterian church; she has been chorister of the church for a number of years.

Rosa Van Lear, daughter of Henry Daniel Smouse, was born July 19, 1863. She was not four years old yet when her father's family moved from Maryland to Washington, Iowa. She was graduated from Washington High school and Academy. She married Charles W. Stephens, a merchant, October 18, 1888. To them were born two children, Ruth, who died in infancy, and Carol E., born October 4, 1898. Their present address is Parsons, Kansas.

Viola May, daughter of John H. Smouse, was born at

Mannington, West Virginia, May 1866, and died at Washington, Iowa, May 17, 1884.

Harry Ulysses, son of John H. Smouse, was born April 26, 1868, at Mannington, West Virginia. He went to Morrison, Illinois, in March 1889. He married Nettie May Clark, October 4, 1894. They have one son, Clark J., born January 15, 1901. Harry is foreman in a factory at Morrison, Ill.

Clifford B., son of John H. Smouse, was born at Mannington, W. Va., October 26, 1869. When quite young he went to Keysville, Maryland. He was married to Florence Walche, January 17, 1899. He is a farmer, and his present address is York Roads, Carroll county, Md.

Ethel, daughter of Leonard, and granddaughter of Henry D. Smouse, was born in Washington, Iowa, October 15, 1874. She was educated in the schools of the city and graduated with honors from both the High school and the Academy. She married Frank H. Wells, a shoe merchant, of Fairfield, Iowa, their present home. She is a member of the Presbyterian church, and P. E. O. Her marriage occurred October 5, 1902.

Edith, daughter of Leonard, and granddaughter of Henry D. Smouse, was born July 11, 1876. She is a graduate of the High school and Academy, of Washington, Iowa. She married John M. Bowman, October 4, 1899, a dry goods merchant of Washington, Ia., their present address. She is a member of the Presbyterian church.

Jessie Belle, daughter of Winfield, and granddaughter of Henry Daniel Smouse, was born at Washington, Iowa, July 14, 1874. She is a graduate of Washington High school, Washington Academy, and Lake Forest Seminary. In the latter institution she carried off the honors of her class. She was married to Ralph E. Daugherty, October 25, 1899, a clothing merchant and real estate dealer. She is an active member of the Presbyterian church and Christian Endeavor

Society. She is also a member of Ferry Hall Alumni Association. Her present address is Washington, Iowa.

Cecil Glenn Conard, son of Amanda, and grandson of Henry D. Smouse, was born August 19, 1887, at Washington, Iowa, where he still resides with his mother.

Florence Ingersoll Smouse, daughter of Arnold, and granddaughter of Henry D. Smouse, was born at Washington, Ia., January 18, 1887. She moved to Mt. Vernon with her parents in 1893. In 1903 she moved with her mother to Syracuse, N. Y., where she now resides.

Arthur Clare Dewey, son of Sarah E., and grandson of Henry D. Smouse, was born at Washington, Ia., September 1, 1886. His residence is at Washington.

Howard Lessing Anderson, son of Mary Virginia, and grandson of Henry D. Smouse, was born at Washington, Ia., January 4, 1894.

Henry Donald Anderson, son of Mary Virginia, and grandson of Henry D. Smouse, was born at Washington, Ia., June 20, 1896.

Carol Stephens, daughter of Rosa Van Lear, and granddaughter of Henry D. Smouse, was born at Washington, Ia., October 4, 1898.

Elizabeth Elma Bowman, daughter of Edith, and granddaughter of Leonard Smouse, was born at Washington, Iowa, December 22, 1900.

David Smouse, son of Henry and grandson of Peter Smouse, was born June 2, 1828, near Cumberland, Md. His boyhood was spent in Allegheny county, Maryland. He was united in marriage to Miss Elnora Brotemarkle, June 27, 1847, by Rev. Peter Riser, at Cumberland, Md. They moved to Iowa City, Iowa, in April 1856, then to Washington, Iowa, in August 1856, where they resided until February 26, 1881, when they moved to Mt. Pleasant, Iowa, their present residence. Five children were born of this union: Emma, the only daughter, deceased; Albert L., of Des Moines, Iowa; Charles W., of Mt. Pleasant, Iowa; David H., of Mt. Pleasant, Ia., William O., deceased. The subject of this sketch is the original patentee of The Smouse Palace Self-Skimming Evaporator, for making fine syrups from all the northern and southern canes, and is known almost world-wide. He is still connected with the "Smouse Manufacturing Co.," Mt. Pleasant, Iowa. Always glad to see any of his friends.

Albert L. Smouse of Des Moines, Ia., is the father of three children, Frank, William O., and Daisy.

Charles Witmer Smouse, son of David, and grandson of Henry Smouse, was born near Frostburg, Maryland, April 19, 1853. When three years old his father moved to Iowa, and the little lad grew to manhood in his adopted state. He was united in marriage to Miss Leila Whisler on December 12, 1882. Residence, Mt. Pleasant, Iowa. Three children were born of this union, Eva Pearl, Aulda Raymond and little Charles Leonard. The subject of this sketch is secretary and treasurer of the Smouse Manufacturing Co., Mt. Pleasant, Ia.

David H. Smouse, son of David and Elnora Smouse, has these children: Earl, Vernal, Olney, Violet and Midge.

William O. Smouse died young.

Odella, daughter of John and Mary Smouse, was born November 4, 1767. She married Henry Koontz, who was born October 4, 1765. She was the mother of these children, viz., John, Eve, Mary, Elizabeth, David, Henry, George, and Sarah.

John Koontz, son of Odella (Smouse) Koontz, was born January 13, 1796. He married Elizabeth Winegardener, and was the father of eight children, viz., William, John, Henry, James, Mary, Peter, Eve and Anna.

Eve Koontz, daughter of Odella (Smouse) Koontz, was born June 17, 1799. She married Philip Mann and had four children, viz., Hannah, Mary, Tillie, and Henry, the son being a noted physician.

Mary Koontz, daughter of Odella (Smouse) Koontz, was born January 9, 1801. She married John Silvers and was the mother of three sons, Richard, Henry, and Asa.

Elizabeth Koontz, daughter of Odella (Smouse) Koontz, was born February 2, 1803. Died August 23, 1887, aged 84 years, 6 months, and 21 days. She was married to Peter Winegardener who was born January 23, 1799. To this union were born 9 children, viz., John, Odella, Henry, William, Margaret, Richard, Sarah, Elizabeth and Annie.

David Koontz, son of Odella (Smouse) Koontz, was born May 20, 1805. He married Eve Wisegarver. No issue.

John Winegardener, son of Peter and Elizabeth, is living in Missouri. No record of family.

Odella, daughter of Peter and Elizabeth (Smouse) Winegardener, married William Philips. Both deceased.

Henry, son of Peter and Elizabeth (Smouse) Winegardener, was born November 22, 1828. He was married to Susan Miller. Five children blessed this union. He died some years ago.

William, son of Peter and Elizabeth (Smouse) Winegardener, married Mary Ann ———. To this union were born five children, viz., John, Anna C., Edmund, Carrie A., and George P.

Margaret, daughter of Peter and Elizabeth (Smouse) Winegardener, married Michael S. Miller. Seven children were born to this union.

Richard Winegardener, son of Peter and Elizabeth, died in youth.

Sarah, daughter of Peter and Elizabeth (Smouse) Winegardener, married Philip Hoover. They have seven children.

Elizabeth, daughter of Peter and Elizabeth (Smouse) Winegardener, married Job Hershberger. Two children were born to this union.

Annie, daughter of Peter and Elizabeth (Smouse) Winegardener, died in infancy.

Henry, son of Henry and Odella (Smouse) Koontz, was born June 4, 1808. He was united in wedlock to Cathrine Hershberger, November 24, 1833. To this union 6 children were born, viz., David, John H., William, Anna M., George Z., and Winfield.

David Koontz, son of Henry Koontz, was born June 1, 1834; died June 18, 1835.

John H., son of Henry, and grandson of Henry and Odella (Smouse) Koontz, was born in Bedford county, Pennsylvania, March 26, 1836. He with his brothers, own the old Homestead of his grandfather who emigrated from Loudoun county, Va., when but few settlers were brave hearted enough to locate in the wilderness. The subject of this sketch has numerous Indian relics in his cabinet of curios. He is a member of "The Historical Committee of the Smouse Association," and has been assiduous and pains-taking in gathering data. He was united in marriage to Mary Moses, Sept. 1, 1859, the Rev. H. Heckerman, officiating. His children are George W., Emma C., and Anna O.

Emma C., daughter of John H. and Mary Koontz, was born June 28, 1863. She was joined in holy wedlock to Jacob H. Zimmers, December 25, 1884. To this union 5 sons were born, viz., John, George, Albert, Clyde and Herbert.

Anna Odella, daughter of John H. and Mary Koontz, was born July 13, 1866. She was united in marriage to Franklin J. Naugle, January 2, 1890. To this union one child was born, Ada Ruth.

William, son of Henry, and grandson of Henry and Odella (Smouse) Koontz, was born February 2, 1838. His

34

grandfather located in the wilds of Bedford county, Pa., having cut a road through the forest until he came to a place which suited him. He (Henry Koontz) lived in his wagon for one year, by which time he had cleared a plot, erected buildings, and was ready for permanent location. The subject of this sketch was born on this farm; here he lived and died. He was married to Susanna Miller, December 19, 1861. To this union three children were born, viz., Henry, who died in infancy, David M., and George W.

David M., son of William and Susanna Koontz, was born April 6, 1864. He married Minnie Anderson and had two children, who died in infancy.

George W., son of William and Susanna Koontz, was born October 14, 1866. He married Annie Diehl and is the father of five children. Two of them died in infancy. The others are Harry, born November 29, 1889; Ethel S., born June 8, 1893; Howard J., born July 5, 1899.

Anna M., daughter of Henry, and granddaughter of Odella (Smouse) Koontz, married Joseph Miller. Her children are George, Elsworth, John, William, Cathrine, Ada deceased, Brice, Anna, and Charles.

George, son of Henry, and grandson of Henry and Odella (Smouse) Koontz, was born April 29, 1845. He married Anna Margaret Wisegarver, February 7, 1867. They had one child, Carrie Koontz, who married Harry Heltzel, January 2, 1890.

Sarah, daughter of Henry and Odella (Smouse) Koontz, was born March 23, 1844. Her certificate of baptism in German script, dated March 31, 1844, is still in her possession. She was married to Jacob Yont. Her children are: John, George, David, Matilda, Jacob and Peter.

John, son of Jacob and Sarah Yont, was born April 17, 1840. He was united in marriage to Margaret Ritchey. Their offspring are Sarah, born October 4, 1868; Annie, born

June 9, 1870; Charles, born February 28, 1873; Daisy, born July 28, 1875; Ada, born February 13, 1879.

George, son of Jacob and Sarah Yont, was born August 25, 1851. He married Maria Koontz, January 22, 1874. One son was born to this union, John H., born July 5, 1877.

David, son of Jacob and Sarah Yont, was born May 27, 1835. He married a lady whose name is unknown to the writer. No record of the family was obtained.

Matilda, daughter of Jacob and Sarah Yont, was born May 1, 1837. She married John Holderbaum. To this union these children were born, viz., Scott, Ellen and Blanche.

Jacob, son of Jacob and Sarah Yont, was born August 20, 1852. He married Rose Koontz, December 25, 1873. His children are Matilda, Maggie, Annie, and Scott.

Peter Yont is single.

Odella Koontz was born May 28, 1817. She married John Brice, November 9, 1852. Mr. Brice was born February 20, 1803; died March 29, 1877. Two children blessed this union, John, born October 9, 1853, and William, born February 8, 1855. John and William were heads of families but the author failed to get the names of their wives. Their children are named as follows: John has these children viz., Charles, Henderson, Minta, Margaret, and John. William's children are William C., Mary Odella, John Smyser, and Albert Clark.

Winfield, son of Henry, and grandson of Odella (Smouse) Koontz, was born March 12, 1849; died September 23, 1902. He was married to Elizabeth Beckley, November 18, 1873. He was the father of three sons: Samuel H., Charles W., and David Berton.

Samuel H., son of Winfield and Elizabeth Koontz, was born in Bedford county, Pa., June 15, 1874. He is a noted musician and has been an instructor in instrumental music for a number of years. He has been married twice, first to

Nellie Holderbaum; second to Myrtle Holderbaum. They were sisters, both deceased.

Charles W., son of Winfield and Elizabeth Koontz, was born May 16, 1878. On August 5, 1902, he married Alice Beckley. Two sons were born to this union, viz., Paul Beckley, born August 15, 1903, and Ross Roosevelt, June 20, 1905.

David Berton, son of Winfield and Elizabeth Koontz, was born January 4, 1887. On November 29, 1906, he was married to Olive Koontz, deceased. They had one son, Francis Clark, born November 10, 1907.

John, son of Daniel and Mary Smouse married Jane Reynolds, of Uniontown, Pa., a daughter of William Reynolds, a hotel keeper in turnpike days, and also the first Adam's Express agent in western Pennsylvania. Four children were born to Mr. and Mrs. Smouse, viz., Mary, Almira, (both dead); Margaret and George.

George, son of John and Jane Smouse, was born August 2, 1865. He was united in marriage to May Torrence, of Pittsburg, Pa., October 10, 1893. To this union three children were born, viz., Morris, (dead); Irene, born November 7, 1896, and Mary, born January 17, 1901. Mr. Smouse is engaged in newspaper work, as head man in the typesetting department of the Chronicle Telegraph.

Margaret, daughter of John and Jane Smouse, was united in marriage to D. G. Scott, of Cumberland, Maryland. Two children bless this union, Ethel and Ruth.

Peter Smouse, son of Peter, had twelve children, viz., Laura, (dead, had five children), Harry, Ernest, Clark, Merrill and Jessie; Emma, has six children, as follows: Maude Young, (two children), Mabel Cole, Annie, Rodger, Emma, and Louisa; Theodore, has six children; Charles, has four children, Nellie, Marion, Albert, and infant; W. H. Smouse, has one son, Murry; Gussie, lives in New Jersey; May Willison, lives in Cumberland, Md.; Sallie Little, lives in Pittsburg, Pa.; J. Neff Smouse, has three children, Hattie, May, and Ralph; Harriet A., (dead); Mary E., (dead); Peter B., is single.

Daniel Smouse, son of Henry Smouse, married Mary Clice. Their children were: William, George, John, Daniel, Thomas, Henry, Samuel, Edward, Joseph, Polly, Louisa, Caroline, Rebecca, Cathrine, and Jane.

George Smouse, son of Daniel Smouse, married a Miss Newman in 1850. To them were born two sons, viz., Daniel and George.

Daniel Smouse, son of George, and grandson of Daniel Smouse, was united in marriage to Mary A. Hichins. To this union the following named children were born, viz., Charles Melvin, born October 16, 1872; Anna May, born March 16, 1875; Jane Frances, born March 18, 1877; George Daniel, born April 11, 1879, died February 21, 1896; Emma Belle, born December 26, 1881; Eva Rosie, born January 23, 1886; Margaret Louisa, born May 21, 1888; Nettie Alma, born March 12, 1891; John Lawrence, born January 11, 1893, and Mary Olive, born October 24, 1895.

Jane Frances Smouse, daughter of Daniel, and granddaughter of George Smouse, married William C. Lehr, of Frostburg, Maryland, September 28, 1903.

Emma Belle Smouse, daughter of Daniel and granddaughter of George Smouse, was married to J. M. Shipley, of Pittsburg, Pa., January 3, 1904.

Daniel, son of Peter Smouse, was born in 1784 and died in 1857.

George, son of Daniel Smouse, was born in 1810 and died in 1855.

William, son of Daniel Smouse, had four sons and two daughters, (all dead).

Henry Smouse, son of Daniel, is in Grantsville, Maryland. No record of his family.

Edward Smouse, son of Daniel, has seven children, viz., John Smouse, who has three boys, Carroll, Harry, and Walter; H. W. Smouse has one boy, Hamill; W. H. Smouse has two boys, Henry and Ralph; Albert Smouse has one girl, Ruth; E. H. Smouse has two boys and one girl, Frank, Oliver, and Ellen; Alice Smouse Eckels has two boys and two girls, viz., Carroll, Paul, Nellie and Edith; Ida Smouse Messenger has four children, viz., Anna, Charles, Lester, and Nellie.

George Adam, son of John and Mary Smouse, moved from Bedford county, Pa., to Plumville, Indiana county, Pa. He had three boys and three girls, viz., James, Adam, Conrad, Mary, Cathrine and Susan, all dead at this writing. The writer was unable to get any data of the children except that of Conrad, who had three children. Their names were not given. The subject of this sketch was in the Revolutionary war for four years and three months, and engaged in many hard fought battles, but was never wounded nor sick during his long and arduous service for independence.

Michael, son of John and Mary Wolphrom Smouse, was born in Loudoun county, Virginia, in 1774. He was twelve years of age when his father moved into Bedford county, Pa., in 1786. He died December 3, 1851, aged 77 years, 2 months and 4 days. He died on the farm now owned and occupied by Henry Smouse. His wife was Sophia Nycum, a native of Loudoun county, Virginia. He was the father of thirteen children, all of whom lived to be over fifty years of age. His children were: John, George, Henry, Jonathan, Michael, Daniel, William, Mary, Cathrine, Annie, Elizabeth, Margaret and Sophia.

John, son of Michael and grandson of John Smouse, was born September 18, 1800. He was united in marriage to Mary Lutz, and they had three children, Rosanna S., George and Mary.

George, son of Michael and grandson of John Smouse, was united in marriage to Eliza Mortimore. Their children are Henry and Lucinda.

Jonathan, son of Michael and grandson of John Smouse, was born February 2, 1806. He died September 6, 1889. He was united in marriage to Miss Mary Ann Whitford. To this union were born nine children, viz., William Harris, was born April 10, 1833; Cathrine Rebecca, and Sophia Elizabeth (twins), were born November 8, 1834. Sophia Elizabeth died April 26, 1836; James Henry, was born April 3, 1837, and died February, 1884; Alexander W., was born May 24, 1839, and died July 23, 1841; Mary L., was born August 18, 1841; Anna A., was born December 28, 1843; Margaret and Martha, (twins) born August 13, 1846.

William Harris, son of Jonathan, and grandson of Michael Smouse, was united in marriage to Sarah Ann Baker, November 23, 1854, and six children were born to this union: John B. Smouse, born October 21, 1855. He married Edna Black, February 26, 1896. He is living at 1364 Washington Boulevard, Chicago, Ill. William J., Ida Belle, Anna Rosecrans, Lora Hattie, and Harriet Mabel.

William Jonathan, son of William Harris, and grandson of Jonathan Smouse, was born December 10, 1857, and was married October 31, 1901, to Gertrude Lawson. He is in the harness and saddlery business with his father.

Ida Belle, daughter of William Harris, and granddaughter of Jonathan Smouse, was born February 13, 1860. She was united in marriage to Judge Thomas McGiberson, September 29, 1881. Issue, one daughter, Belle Giberson, born March 16, 1883.

Anna Rosecrans, daughter of William Harris, and granddaughter of Jonathan Smouse, was born September 29, 1862.

Lora Hattie Smouse, was born October 9, 1866, and died August 2, 1867.

Harriet Mabel, daughter of William Harris, and granddaughter of Jonathan Smouse, was born August 9, 1871.

William Harris Smouse and family moved from Somerset county, Pa., to Lee county, Ill., April 1856. He rented a farm four years and tilled the soil for that period of time, when he sold out and moved to Cedar Rapids, Iowa, and engaged in the harness business with his father until his enlistment in the 24th Iowa Volunteer Infantry, August 13, 1862. He was mustered into the United States service at Muscatine, Iowa, September 18, 1862, as corporal, Company G., 24th Iowa, promoted to Quarter-Master Sergeant, June 23, 1863. He was promoted to First Lieutenant and Adjutant, December 16, 1864. He served under General U. S. Grant, in the Vicksburg campaign, with General Banks on the Red river and General Phil. Sheridan in the Shenendoah Valley, Virginia, when he made his famous ride, October 19, 1864, and turned defeat into victory at Cedar Creek. He was mustered out of service at Savannah, Georgia, July 17, 1865. He returned home, August 4, 1865. He is now engaged in the wholesale manufacture of harness and saddlery, under the firm name of Smouse & Son, Cedar Rapids, Iowa.

Cathrine Rebecca, daughter of Jonathan, and granddaughter of Michael Smouse, was born November 8, 1834. She was married to Will Johnson for her first husband and had one child, Edward Johnson. She was united in marriage to J. A. Benner, as her second husband, and to this union were born the following named children: Robert and Mary. Mrs. J. A. Benner now resides at 771 East 6th street, Portland, Oregon. Mary Benner, daughter of J. A. and Cathrine Benner, married Edgar Simmons and has two children. Names not given.

Anna A., daughter of Jonathan and granddaughter of Michael Smouse, was united in marriage to Will Hawks, and their home is at Nye, Montana.

Martha McClintock, daughter of Jonathan and granddaughter of Michael Smouse, was born August 13, 1845. She was united in marriage to Thomas Chiverton. To this union were born two girls, Fanny and Bertha. They reside at 627 A. avenue, West Cedar Rapids, Iowa.

George, son of Michael and Sophia Smouse, was born December 10, 1802, and died January 23, 1885. He was united in marriage to Eliza Mortimore, who was born May 23, 1813, and died March 22, 1874. To this union two children were born, Henry and Lucinda.

Henry, son of George and grandson of Michael Smouse, was born June 6, 1837. He was united in marriage to Mary Weyand April 3, 1873, and an only son was born to bless this union, George Ellis, born June 5, 1874, who has been employed by the U. S. navy, as a machinist. He is in Washington, D. C., where he has been for several years.

Lucinda, daughter of George and Eliza Smouse, was born April 6, 1839. She was united in marriage to Daniel B. Deihl, December 25, 1867. To this union were born a son and a daughter, Elmer and Ella.

Ella Deihl was born December 23, 1868, and married Plummer James, June 16, 1897. No issue.

Elmer Deihl was born June 18, 1870 and married Blanche Deihl June 16, 1897. Issue: Esta M., Glenn, Eugene and Ella.

Annie, daughter of Michael, and granddaughter of John Smouse, was united in wedlock to William States. To this union were born four boys and four girls: Simon, Franklin, Thomas, William, Mary, Louisa, Sophia and Sarah.

Elizabeth, daughter of Michael, and granddaughter of John Smouse, was united in marriage to William Defibaugh. Eleven children were born to this union, viz., David, Lawrence, Wesley, Milton, William, Sophia, Mary, Belle, Kate, Eliza, and Clara.

Sophia Defibaugh was married, but the writer did not learn to whom, as the "data" simply stated that she was the mother of seven children, viz., Lucinda, Shunk, Chinoweth, Michael, Shannon, Daniel and Alexander. It is unfortunate that complete data could not be obtained, so the family could be fully described in this work.

John, son of Michael and Sophia Smouse, was born July 18, 1800. He married Mary Cathrine Lutz, and unto this union were born three children, viz., Rosannah, George, and Mary. He died June 6, 1868, aged 76 years, 4 months, and 27 days. His wife died, aged 64 years.

Rosannah, daughter of John, and granddaughter of Michael Smouse, was born November 11, 1826, and died November 25, 1905, aged 79 years and 14 days. She was never married.

George, son of John, and grandson of Michael Smouse, was born in Snake Spring township, Bedford county, Pa., on July 12, 1833. He was united in marriage to Maria Grove, who was born February 21, 1836. To this union were born the following named children: John W., Thomas F., Sarah E., Mary C., George E., Harry L., Rosa B., Ada M. and Anna V. The last two are twins. Mr. Smouse was married February 22, 1854. His wife died September 17, 1889. He married Mrs. Mary Beegle, April 20, 1892, as his second wife. Her maiden name was Fluke. She was born May 25, 1848.

Mary, daughter of John, and granddaughter of Michael Smouse, was united in marriage to Wesley Hartzell, August 4, 1858. To this union two children were born, Anna Virginia, born August 19, 1859. She was married to Godfrey Rusher, in February, 1884. John Hartzell was born October 30, 1861, and was married to Clara Kuhn in June 1902. Wesley Hartzell died in the fall of 1863. Mary Hartzell nee Smouse was united in marriage to George Koontz, January

10, 1867. To this union four children were born, Mary Kathryn, born November 12, 1867; Emma Valeria, born June 15, 1869; Warren Sangree, born April 22, 1878; Edith Sarah, born October 8, 1880.

Mary Kathryn Koontz was united in marriage to Charles Elder, February 16, 1896. To this union four children were born, viz., Edith, born December 12, 1896; George, born April 19, 1898; Mary, born June 9, 1903, and Joseph, born October 8, 1905.

Emma Valeria Koontz is single and at home.

Warren Sangree Koontz was united in marriage to Edith Triplett, July 30, 1901. To this union were born two children, viz., Raymond, born October 6, 1902, and Verna, born August 9, 1905.

Edith Sarah Koontz, was united in marriage to Walter Fletcher, November 27, 1907.

John W., son of George, and grandson of John Smouse, was born near Lutzville, Bedford county, Pa., December 28, 1855. He was united in marriage to Miss Susan Ford, of Cypher, Pa., November 19, 1879. His wife was born May 8, 1860. To this union were born three sons and five daughters, viz., Carrie Elizabeth, born August 31, 1880; Charles Walter, born April 19, 1882; George Edgar, born January 21, 1884; Ethel Maria, born May 26, 1885; Mary Virginia, born February 11, 1890; Fanny Ruth, born May 27, 1892; Susan Grace, born May 5, 1894; John Michael, born June 14, 1896.

George Edgar, son of John W. and Susan Smouse, was united in marriage to Miss Cloe Morehead. One son was born to this union, George Raymond.

Carrie, Charles, Ethel, Mary, Fanny, Grace and John, are at home.

Thomas F. Smouse, son of George, and grandson of John Smouse, was born December 23, 1857, near Lutzville, Pa. He attended the public schools of his native county and district, and a six weeks' course at Bedford Normal school, qualified him to teach. He began teaching when 16 years old, and taught for five consecutive terms. He engaged in the lumber business in June, 1889, at Cumberland, Maryland, which business he still follows. He was elected a member of council in his adopted city and served from June 1904 to June 1906, and refused a re-election to devote his time to his business, which was necessarily neglected while in council. He was elected President of the "Smouse Association of America," September 6, 1899, which office he has held ever since, being re-elected annually. He was united in marriage to Miss Annie R. Beegle, December 20, 1882. She was a daughter of Joseph F. Beegle, a prosperous and prominent farmer of Friends Cove, Bedford county, Pa., and she was born June 21, 1856. Two children were born to Mr. and Mrs. Smouse, viz., Cora E., a graduate of Kee Mar College, June 1907, at the age of 20 years. She is now assistant principal in the High school at North East, Cecil county, Maryland. Their son Thomas R., now near 18 years old, is a graduate of the Tri-State Business College of Cumberland, and is bookkeeper and general office clerk for his father.

George E., son of George, and grandson of John Smouse, was born near Lutzville, Pa. He was married to Mary Heavner. One son was born to this union, when death claimed the devoted wife and mother. He now resides at Terra Alta, W. Va.

Harry L., son of George, and grandson of John Smouse, was born near Lutzville, Pa. He was married to Sadie French. No issue. Mr. Smouse lives at Albright, W. Va.

Sarah E., daughter of George, and granddaughter of John Smouse, was united in marriage to Isaiah Beegle. To them were born these children: Walter, Harry, Ada, Charles, and Isaiah. Mr. Beegle died and the widow married John Diehl, by whom she had two children, Norman and Floyd.

Mary C., daughter of George, and granddaughter of John Smouse, was united in marriage to Shannon Beegle. To this union were born these children: George E., Lester, and Harvey.

Rosa B., daughter of George, and granddaughter of John Smouse, was born near Lutzville, Pa. She now lives at New Boston, Illinois. She is married to Otis Randolph. They have no issue.

Ada M., daughter of George, and granddaughter of John Smouse, was united in marriage to Joshua Deihl. These children were born to this union: Ruth, Marsha, and Mary Pearl.

Annie V., daughter of George, and granddaughter of John Smouse, was married to Edward Deihl and had two children, Everett and Rozella. She was divorced, and married William Teeman, of Joy, Illinois. Issue, Henry and infant.

Margaret S., daughter of Jonathan, and granddaughter of Michael Smouse, was born August 13, 1845. She married Mack Davis, and has six children. Their present address is Bolis, Nebraska.

Henry, son of Michael, and grandson of John Smouse, was united in marriage to Polly States. To this union were born four children, Josiah, James, Sarah and Margaret. Both sons served in the Civil War from 1862 to 1865.

Daniel, son of Michael, and grandson of John Smouse, was united in marriage to Lydia Roland, March 19, 1842. To this union were born Simon, David, John, Eliza, Lucinda, William, Joseph and Philip, (twins), Sophia and Emma.

Simon, son of Daniel and Lydia Smouse, was born August 29, 1843. He is a noted musician and a prominent member of society. He was married July 24, 1866, to Mary M. Oler, who was born June 29, 1845. Their children are: Eliza

V., who is single; Alice, married Carl C. Clippinger, and has three children, William, Fred, and Mary.

James W., son of Simon and Mary Smouse, was united in marriage to Minnie Garritson. Louisa is single, and so is Esther.

Thomas Edgar, son of Simon Smouse, was married to Cassie Laughner and has one child, Frank Edgar.

David, son of Daniel and Lydia Smouse, served during the Civil War. He returned home after Lee's surrender, shattered in body, and died soon after reaching home.

John, son of Daniel and Lydia Smouse, was united in marriage to Drusilla Evans, March 15, 1876. To this union were born fourteen children, viz., Alverta Fern, born December 8, 1877, at Paw Paw, W. Va.; Georgiana Mae, born September 29, 1879; Daniel James, born February 3, 1881, and died July 7, 1881; Emma Virginia, born June 4, 1882, and died July 23, 1882; Lydia Violet, born November 4, 1883, and died June 12, 1891; Alta Neola, born January 17, 1885; Dessie Margaret, born September 3, 1886; Josiah Alpheus and William Harrison were born September 9, 1889, and William Harrison died June 7, 1890; Flora Lorean, born February 18, 1892; Mary Etta, born March 15, 1894; Howard Christian, born August 17, 1897; Ethel Marie and Edna DeOlva, born November 29, 1899.

Mae Smouse was married to Mr. P. Stokes, December 28, 1903. One son, Harold, was born to this union, September 9, 1904.

Lucinda, daughter of Daniel and Lydia Smouse, was united in marriage to L. S. Hawn. To this union were born six sons, viz., Milton, Edgar, Atley, Walter, Albert, and John.

Milton, son of Lucinda (Smouse) Hawn, was married to Jennie Adams. To this union one child was born, Mary M. Mr. Hawn died soon after the birth of his daughter.

Edgar, son of Lucinda (Smouse) Hawn, was married to Cathrine Replogle. No children.

Atley, son of Lucinda (Smouse) Hawn, married Frances B. Fisher. To this union one child was born, Dorothy B.

John, son of Lucinda (Smouse) Hawn, died when young, and her son, Walter, is still at home.

William, son of Daniel and Lydia Smouse, was born at Everett, Pa., January 20, 1857. He married Miss Mary Louisa Fleming, of Marseilles, Ill., June 6, 1900. Miss Fleming was born October 18, 1869. To this union one son was born, Wilbur Fleming Smouse.

Sophia, daughter of Daniel and Lydia Smouse, married Lem Wilger, a locomotive engineer on the P. R. R. To them were born two sons, Edward and Francis.

Emma, daughter of Daniel and Lydia Smouse, married John Burley, of State Line. One son was born to bless this union, Stephen Burley.

William, son of Michael, and grandson of John Smouse, was born three miles west of Everett, Pa., April 27, 1825. He was the youngest of thirteen children. He lived at Everett all his life, a millwright by trade. He has built not only many mills, but threshing machines, and also worked at pattern making. He was united in marriage to Hannah Gilliam, and has two children, Sophia and Charles.

Sophia, married Sheridan Leach. Issue: William, Daisy, Percy, and Raymond.

Charles married Violet Barndollar. Issue, Alverda.

Michael, son of Michael, and grandson of John Smouse, was born December 25, 1814. He married Elizabeth Hinish, and had nine children, James F., Mary C., Sophia, Eliza B., Henrietta, Clara, Emma, William and John.

Mary, daughter of Michael and Elizabeth Smouse, was married to George Woodcock, deceased. No issue.

Eliza B., daughter of Michael Smouse, was united in marriage to Michael Ott, of Everett, Pa.

Sophia, Henrietta, William, and John are all single. William is in Alaska, and John is in Cumberland.

Clara, daughter of Michael Smouse, married John Derenzy, of Denver, Colorado.

Mary, daughter of Michael, and granddaughter of John Smouse, was united in marriage to William Nycum, and two sons and two daughters were born to this union. John Nycum, of Mann's Choice, Pa., and William Nycum, of Broken Bow, Colorado.

Sophia, daughter of Mary Smouse Nycum, was married to John Betz. No record of family.

Emma, daughter of Mary Smouse Nycum, and granddaughter of Michael Smouse, was united in wedlock to Rev. Nehemiah Skyles, of the Reformed church. To this union were born six children, viz., Ella, Eugene P., William N., Harry H., Russel, and Charles.

Ella Skyles married J. W. Martin. Issue, John S. Martin.

Eugene P. Skyles, married Mary Johnson and has one child. He was ordained a minister in the Reformed church, and is located at Cumberland, Maryland.

William N. Skyles, son of Emma Nycum Skyles, is married, but the writer failed to learn the lady's name.

Harry H. Skyles is single and is in Brooklyn, N. Y.

Russel Skyles is single, a druggist, Brooklyn, N. Y.

Charles Skyles is still at home.

Cathrine, daughter of Michael, and granddaughter of John Smouse, was united in marriage to John Mortimore. To this union were born four sons and three daughters, viz., Josiah, Alexander, William, Wesley, Elizabeth, Mary and Isabell.

Margaret, daughter of Michael, and granddaughter of

John Smouse, was born April 20, 1820. She was united in marriage to Dewalt Hershberger, February 17, 1842. These children were born to this union: Henry, born April 29, 1843; Rebecca, born September 28, 1844; David, born September 4, 1846; Samuel, born November 22, 1851; William, born August 18, 1854; Franklin, born January 26, 1858; Mary C., born September 4, 1863.

Henry R., son of Dewalt and Margaret (Smouse) Hershberger, was born April 29, 1843. He was married to Margaret Carney, December 25, 1873. Miss Carney was born July 2, 1846, and died March 31, 1884. One child was born to this union, viz., Minnie. B. His second marriage was with Margaret Lessig, July 21, 1888. To this union five children were born, viz., Margaret McFadden, born September 16, 1889, and died December 27, 1898; John H., born April 7, 1891; Ella M., born December 21, 1893; Paul H., born October 7, 1896; Gerald W., born April 23, 1901, and died May 28, 1902.

Anna Mary Harclerode, daughter of Henry and Fanny (Smouse) Harclerode, was born October 8, 1856, and married James A. Points. Issue, Mary Grace Points. Mrs. Points is a sister of J. P. Harclerode, owner of the old John Smouse farm at Ashcom, Pa.

William, son of Dewalt and Margaret (Smouse) Hershberger, was born August 18, 1854, and married Sarah Shatzer, August 24, 1881. To this union were born seven children, viz., Mae, born November 12, 1882; Nellie, born February 1, 1884; Emma, born May 14, 1885; James, born August 7, 1887; William E., born July 20, 1889; Frank W., born October 27, 1892, and Ruth A., born July 23, 1895.

Nellie, daughter of William, and granddaughter of Margaret (Smouse) Hershberger, was united in marriage to Harry Zimmers, February 27, 1907.

William Smouse, son of George, was united in marriage

to Barbara Smith. To this union were born four daughters and one son, viz., Mary, Hannah, Elizabeth, Nancy and George.

Mary Smouse, daughter of William, was united in marriage to Andrew Baker, and these children were born to this union: William, Melda, John, George, Ellen, Harry, Frank, and Nancy.

William Baker, son of Mary (Smouse) Baker, married Nettie Bowser. His children are Nelson, Lizzie, Mary, and John.

Melda Baker, daughter of Mary (Smouse) Baker, married Simon Kauffman. Her children are Mabel, Marie, and Ralph.

John Baker, son of Mary (Smouse) Baker, married Miss Mary E. Spiece. His children are Mary, Walter, Clifford, Jeanette and Kenneth.

George Baker, son of Mary (Smouse) Baker, married Ledora Arthur. His children are Ruth, Mary, and Floretta. One child died in infancy.

Ellen and Harry Baker, children of A. N. and Mary Baker, are still single.

Frank, son A. N. and Mary (Smouse) Baker, married Miss Rebecca Stuckey.

Nancy, daughter of A. N. and Mary (Smouse) Baker, was born June 3, 1876. She was united in marriage to Albert H. Stoner, July 6, 1898. Mr. Stoner was born January 16, 1872. He worked on his father's farm until he was seventeen years of age. At that age he engaged as a clerk with Eichelberger, Earlenbaugh Co., serving in that capacity for five years. He then engaged in the grocery business for himself and has been eminently successful. He is now serving his ninth year as councilman of his home town, Martinsburg, Pa. To Mr. and Mrs. Stoner, are born these children: Gilbert B., born August 26, 1899; Raymond R., born August 4, 1902; Albert

H., born September 10, 1904; M. Marjorie, born October 18, 1905.

Hannah, daughter of William and Barbara Smouse, was united in marriage to Theodore D. Snowberger, December 25, 1873. To this union one daughter was born. Miss Ada Snowberger, born August, 20, 1875.

Elizabeth, daughter of William and Barbara Smouse, married Alexander Barnett. To this union were born these children: Hannah, Samuel, Ida, Marie, Clarence, Irvin, Arthur, Roy and Ray.

Hannah is married and has three children.

Samuel is married and has one child.

Ida and Marie are dead.

Clarence, Irvin, Arthur, Roy, and Ray are single.

Nancy, daughter of William and Barbara Smouse, married Samuel Zimmerman, and had these children: William, Minnie, Annie, David and Mary. Her husband died, and after a widowhood of several years, she married Daniel Burket. To this union one son was born, viz., Harry S. Burket.

William Zimmerman, son of Nancy (Smouse) Zimmerman, married Nora Kensinger. Issue, George, Mary, Jacob, Lester and Grace.

Minnie, daughter of Nancy (Smouse) Zimmerman, married Frederick Kauffman. No issue.

Annie, daughter of Nancy (Smouse) Zimmerman, married Edward Bridenbaugh. She had six children. Names not given in data.

David, son of Nancy (Smouse) Zimmerman, married Minnie Hall. He has three children.

Mary, daughter of Nancy (Smouse) Zimmerman, married Albert Kauffman. No issue.

George Smouse, son of William and Barbara Smouse, married Nancy Detwiler, for his first wife. No issue to them. For his second wife he married Mary Replogle. Two children were born to her, when she died, viz., Virginia and Harry. He then married Nancy Replogle, a sister to his second wife. To this last wife two children were born, viz., Jesse and Mary. Harry and Jesse are dead.

George Smouse, son of George Smouse, married Jean Carper and has one child.

Matilda Smouse, daughter of George Smouse, married Robert Elder. To this union were born nine children, viz., Mary, Josiah, George, William, Henry, Isaac, Daniel, John, and Matilda.

Mary Elder, daughter of Matilda (Smouse) Elder, was married three times. Her first husband was John Nicodemus. By him she had two children. Her second husband was John Stuckey. By him she had two children. Her third marriage was to August Shaffer. No issue.

Josiah and George are dead.

William Elder, son of Robert and Matilda (Smouse) Elder, was married twice. For his first wife he married Cathrine Keagy, and had one child. His second marriage was to Kate Carper. To this union no children were born.

Isaac Elder, son of Robert and Matilda (Smouse) Elder, married Maria Stoler. No issue.

Daniel, son of Robert and Matilda (Smouse) Elder, was married and had two children. His wife's maiden name was not given in the data.

John and Robert, sons of Robert and Matilda (Smouse) Elder, are both single.

Matilda, daughter of Robert and Matilda (Smouse) Elder, was united in marriage to John Freeland. No issue.

David Smouse, son of John and Mary Smouse, was united in marriage to Mary Wineland. To this union were born five sons and seven daughters, viz., Jacob, Elizabeth, Mary, Susan, Cathrine, John, Barbary, David, Michael, Nancy, Eve, and Frederick. The subject of this sketch was the fourth son, and like his elder brothers, was very patriotic. His brothers, Peter and George A., were in the Revolutionary war. He was in the War of 1812. He and his brother Michael were at Pittsburg with their teams, having taken merchandise from Baltimore to the city on the Ohio, on their return to Fort Bedford, now Bedford, Pa., they engaged with the government and drove their own teams, until peace was declared, when they returned to their farms in Friends Cove, Bedford county, Pa. His brother, George A., owned a distillery at that time, and he had loaded fifteen barrels of apple jack to be taken to Baltimore, when the news reached him that a squad of soldiers were in the community taking every horse fit for service. His hired man, Mr. H. A. Hill, had just harnessed six horses, when the soldiers were seen coming over the bridge. Instantly he mounted the saddle horse, as he was then called, and driving the others ahead, he swam them across the river, took to the mountains, and thereby saved the horses. The apple jack never reached Baltimore, but it did reach the stomach of many a weary soldier.

Jacob, son of David, and grandson of John Smouse, was a Hercules for his years. When but sixteen years old, he was apprenticed to a man in Everett, Pa., to learn the tanner's trade. The man was abusive and mean. No one could please him, and one day tanner's oil was needed. He sent Jacob to Bedford, a distance of eight miles, to get a jug of oil. Having to pass through the "Narrows" where the river cuts through Tussey's mountain, he hid the jug, went to a friend in Friend's Cove, remained all night, left the following morning, and has never been seen or heard of, from that eventful day to the present. It was during the second month of his apprenticeship, he in company with a friend, went to what was then known as the stone tavern, east of Everett several miles, and being on the Philadelphia and

Pittsburg pike, the house was patronized by the teamsters who were on this thoroughfare. It happened that Charles Mench, a teamster, and a pugilist or slugger, so called in those days, was at the bar when Smouse and his friend entered the door. He said to them, "Stranger, you can come in, but that young snot, (meaning Jacob Smouse), cannot enter or be in here while I am here." Smouse says to Mench, "I am in, and it will take a better man than you, or any other one here to put me out, and more than that, you called me a name for which you must apologize. I never had a quarrel or fight in my life, and you are a man and fighter, and I am a mere boy in years, but your superior in manners, in strength, and in behavior, and you must apologize or I will compel you to do so." Mench laid off his coat and vest, and said to those in the room: "Form a ring and I will show that young jack-a-napes that Charles Mench is the best man between Philadelphia and Pittsburg. Smouse buttoned his coat, walked into the ring, and the contest began. The writer of this sketch has it from an eye witness, who said that when Smouse struck his first blow, he took his antagonist clean off his feet, and that the blood flew to the ceiling of the room. The fight lasted forty-five minutes, and during all this time Mr. Mench never reached Mr. Smouse to give him a scratch. Mr. Mench not only apologized for his rudeness, but declared that Smouse was the best man in America.

Elizabeth, daughter of David and granddaughter of John Smouse, was united in marriage to John Defibaugh. They had no children. She lived to round out 97 years.

Mary, daughter of David and granddaughter of John Smouse, was united in marriage to William F. Defibaugh. He was a brother of John and George Defibaugh; three brothers married three sisters. William and Mary (Smouse) Defibaugh had one child, Mary A. Defibaugh, who was married to Andrew Koontz, both dead. They had no issue.

John, son of David and Mary Smouse, was born May 28, 1802. He was first united in marriage to Elizabeth Glass, and had one son and one daughter born unto them, Abner and Elizabeth. For his second wife he married Elizabeth Maugle, born October 12, 1817. To this union were born these children: Delilah, Mary Ann, Lovina, Levi, Cathrine, Daniel, David, George, Annie, Sarah, John M., Frederick and Andrew (twins), Julia Ann and Elizabeth.

Elizabeth, of the first wife, and Annie, Sarah, Julia Ann and Elizabeth of second wife, all died in youth. The mother of the above named children died May 11, 1874, and the father in January, 1882.

Abner G., son of John and Elizabeth Smouse, was born October 17, 1834. He was united in marriage to Ann Rebecca Carson, January 5, 1860. To this union were born the following named children: Jeremiah, Mary, Barbary Ellen, Samuel D., Harriet Ann, Sarah Jane, Elmira May and William Grant. Jeremiah and Mary died in infancy.

Barbary Ellen, daughter of Abner and Rebecca Smouse was united in marriage to John H. Coy June 4, 1882. These children were born to this union: Jeremiah, Gertrude, Maggie, B., Minnie, Wealthy, Lena, Emery and Esther. Alta and Abner. Jeremiah, Gertrude and Wealthy are dead. Maggie was married to James S. Hart August 12, 1907. The others are all single and at home.

Samuel David, son of Abner and Rebecca Smouse was married to Lizzie Rinehard and to them were born three sons—James C., Isaac H. and Harvey. The first and second named are dead, also the father, Samuel D. Smouse.

Harriet Ann, daughter of Abner and granddaughter of John and Elizabeth Smouse, was united to Elmer S. Burket in the bonds of matrimony April 20, 1890. To this union have been born four sons and three daughters—James Roy, Lloyd S. Elias Clark, Elizabeth Rebecca, Harold Elmer, Flora

Bell and Dorothy May. James Roy and Lloyd S. are both dead.

Sarah Jane, daughter of Abner and Rebecca Smouse, was married to Elias Reed. These two daughters were born unto this union: Florence I., now dead, and Sarah J. The subject of this sketch is also dead.

Elmira May, daughter of Abner and Rebecca Smouse, was married to Reuben Benner in 1892. Her husband died soon after their marriage. In May, 1894, she was united in marriage to John Reed. To this union the following named children were born: Effie B., August 30, 1895, Vera J., July 17, 1898, Anna, September 11, 1900, Ora E., August 22, 1902, Eli, October 10, 1904, Maggie R., December 25, 1906.

William Grant, son of Abner and Rebecca Smouse, a barber by trade, is located at Saxton, Pa. He is married to Bertha Core and has four children, Mary, Elvin, Helen and Ada.

Delilah, daughter of John and Elizabeth Smouse, was united in marriage to James Rhoads and had three children, George, Daniel and Lizzie. The writer received no data as to the families of George and Daniel. Lizzie was united in marriage to Samuel Hartman and bore him three children— Margaret, Lizzie and Jacob.

Margaret Hartman married Homer Albright and has one child.

Lizzie Hartman married Warren Zook and has one child.

Jacob Hartman married Myra Ott in January, 1907. He was in the employ of the Pennsylvania Railroad as car repairer. One morning through the carelessness of a switchman he was crushed to death while under a car. Thus after a few months of wedded life his young wife was left to mourn him whom she loved so well. He was a member of W. C.

Lysinger Castle No. 99, K. G. E., which order had charge of his funeral.

Mary Ann, daughter of John and Elizabeth Smouse, was united in marriage to David B. Kensinger June 1, 1856, and these children, all boys, were born unto them: Ephriam, who died young. Levi, Andrew, John, Frank, Reuben and David.

Mr. D. B. Kensinger died March 26, 1908.

Levi, son of David and Mary A. Kensinger, was married to Mary Beach and had nine children—Ora, married to Harry Furry. Daniel, Dora, Elmer, Maggie, Eddie, Mabel, Flora and Harry.

Daniel and Dora are dead.

Andrew, son of David and Mary A. Kensinger, married Susie Helley and has one child, Mary.

John S., son of David and Mary A. Kensinger, married Hattie Stoner. One child was born unto this union when the wife died. This child is Miss Lena Kensinger. For his second wife he married Amelia Gorsuch. No issue.

Frank S., son of David and Mary A. Kensinger, married Ella Hartzwick. No issue.

Reuben S., son of David and Mary A. Kensinger, married Susie Olbert. To this union three children were born— Earl, Ruth and infant.

David S., son of David and Mary A. Kensinger, married Annie Bowser. One child born to this union.

Lovina, daughter of John and Elizabeth Smouse, born November 2, 1838, married Levi Smeltzer October 18, 1863, who was born April 4, 1824. To this union four children were born—David, Mary E., Keziah E. and Minnie L. Mr. Smeltzer died August 19, 1907.

David Smeltzer, son of Levi and Lovina Smeltzer, born April 4, 1863, married Ella Gorsuch, who was born June 19, 1866. To this union four children are born—Chas. F., Margaret L., Levi H. and Anna E.

Mary E., daughter of Levi and Lovina Smeltzer, born July 25, 1864, married Christian Seedenberg November 19, 1882. To this union were born these children: Oden, born August 6, 1883. Ella L., born February 22, 1886. Levi H., born October 7, 1896. Mrs. Seedenberg died December 9, 1904.

Keziah E., daughter of Levi and Lovina Smeltzer, born January 29, 1866, married Simeon Saulsbury July 3, 1888. To this union were born five children—Oscar, Levi D., Eva, Hazel and Charles.

Minnie L., daughter of Levi and Lovina Smeltzer, born February 26, 1876, married Charles A. Goodwin February 2, 1902. One son born to this union—Claude B.

Levi Smouse, son of John and Elizabeth Smouse, was born October 2, 1841. He was united in wedlock to Hannah Wineland July 5, 1862. To this union were born the following named children: Reuben, Elizabeth, David J., Sophia, Daniel H., John E., Cathrine, Anna and Levi. Mr. Smouse died aged 58 years.

Elizabeth, daughter of Levi and Hannah Smouse, was born September 7, 1865. She was married to Harry Rascher December 2, 1886. Two children were born to this union Hannah Sophia, and Caroline Grace. Mrs. Rascher died February 5, 1892.

Reuben, son of Levi and Hannah Smouse, was born October 14, 1863. He was wedded to Eloise Wise June 12, 1907.

David J., son of Levi and Hannah Smouse, was born December 25, 1867. He was married to ——— —————. Has two boys.

Sophia, daughter of Levi and Hannah Smouse, was born July 14, 1870. She married Harry Hunter, an engineer on the Pennsylvania Railroad.

Daniel H., John E. and Levi J. Smouse died in infancy.

Cathrine, daughter of Levi and Hannah Smouse, was born October 27, 1875. She married John Irvin Dilling November 19, 1893. To this union these children were born: Earl H., Eva May, Emma R. and Esther P.

Anna, daughter of Levi and Hannah Smouse, was born November 8, 1880. She is still single. She is clerking in a department store in Pittsburg, Pa.

Cathrine, daughter of John and Elizabeth Smouse, was married first to George Smith and had four children—Elmer, Harriet, Annie and Andrew. She married James Showalter for her second husband. Had one son, Solomon Showalter, now dead.

Daniel, son of John and Elizabeth Smouse, was born November 11, 1845. He was married to Elizabeth Dilling, in Benton county, Iowa, July 29, 1867. To this union were born three children—Maggie, Minnie J. and John H. Maggie died in infancy and her mother, Elizabeth Smouse, died December 26, 1877. For his second wife Daniel Smouse married Hattie Stewart of Vinton, Benton county, Iowa. To this union four children were born—Charles Delbert, January 10, 1885. Carl C., November 1, 1887. Clark Tilford, ————, 1889 and Vernia Marie March 2, 1896.

David M., son of John and Elizabeth Smouse, was born March 29, 1847. He was married to Mary L. Crofford December 25, 1873, at 2.30 p. m., by Elder S. A. Moore in the home of the minister at New Enterprise, Pa. To this union two sons were born—Sheldon Raymond April 21, 1876, and William A., March 30, 1881.

Sheldon R., son of David and Mary Smouse, married Maud C. Glenn June 29, 1898. To this union were born four children—Kathleen, born March 24, 1899. Caroline, born April 9, 1900. Sheldon R., born September 19, 1901, and David G., born March 9, 1904.

George, son of John and Elizabeth Smouse, was born

April 4, 1849. He went to Benton county, Iowa, in February, 1867, where he was married to Lovina A. Stewart, November 12, 1868. To this union were born Lovina E., September 17, 1869. Leah May, June 7, 1871. John Price, July 23, 1873, and Nettie, August 6, 1880. His wife, Lovina A., died January 29, 1889. He married for his second wife Mabel Cater September 20, 1893. One child was born to this union—Naomi Mabel, born October 31, 1899.

Lovina E., daughter of George and Lovina A. Smouse, was united in marriage to Marion S. Sutton, Rev. J. G. Stewart officiating, December 11, 1889. To this union are born the following named children: Ione Marie, born July 24, 1891. Marion Louise, born August 6, 1896. Esther Louella, born September 13, 1899. Sylvester George, born March 19, 1901.

John Price, son of George and Lovina Smouse, was married to Cathrine E. Nobholz April 18, 1895. To this union were born Robert E., March 7, 1896, Weldon, Laura and Paul P.

John M., son of John and Elizabeth Smouse, was born July 8, 1855. He was united in marriage to Mary Ann Glass Nov. 18, 1875, Henry Nicodemus, of Martinsburg, Pa., performing the ceremony. These children were born to this union: Anna Nora, born March 6, 1875. Ella Jane, born November 10, 1876. Andrew J., July 10, 1882. Daniel G., April 29, 1885. David H. born June 2, 1888, died October 5, 1890. George E., born October 1, 1890, and Mary Edna, born November 10, 1893.

Frederick M., son of John and Elizabeth Smouse, was born September 17, 1858. He was united in marriage to Rachael Lovina Falknor May 29, 1883, who was born June 22, 1859. To this union were born Minnie J., born August 24, 1883, died March 10, 1896. Lena M., born September 15, 1885, died March 16, 1896. Mary E., born September 29, 1898. Harry H., born August 26, 1899.

Andrew M., son of John and Elizabeth Smouse, was born September 17, 1858. (He and Frederick are twins.) He was united in marriage to Lydia Stoner January 1, 1885. To this union one son was born—Howard S. Smouse, born April 3, 1886, and died February 2, 1888. Mrs. Lydia Smouse was born March 2, 1863.

Mr. Smouse has followed threshing for the past twenty-five years. He was elected Treasurer of the Smouse Association at its organization and has been reelected annually ever since. He has the respect, good will and confidence of each and all.

Susan, daughter of David and granddaughter of John Smouse, was united in marriage to George Long. To this union were born one son and one daughter—George and Eve. George served with distinction in Company A, 125th Regiment Pennsylvania Volunteer Infantry. He was wounded at Antietam in that fierce conflict. He died in 1867. Eve Long died aged 20 years.

Cathrine, daughter of David and granddaughter of John Smouse, was united in marriage to Samuel Daugherty. To this union there were two children—Joseph and Mary.

Joseph, son of Cathrine Daugherty and grandson of David Smouse, was born August 16, 1846. He was united in marriage to Rachael Chamberlain. The following named children were born to this union: John W., born September 30, 1867. Mary C., born July 21, 1870. Wrilia J., born February 3, 1873. Mahlon, born March 21, 1875. Henry O., born February 19, 1877. Marshall, born January 15, 1881. Rufus, born August 9, 1884. Bland S., born July 27, 1886. Alice M., born March 3, 1889. Mahlon Daugherty died October 9, 1887.

Mary J., daughter of Samuel and Cathrine (Smouse) Daugherty, was born January 19, 1849. She was united in marriage to Adam Loose. One son was born to this union—

Samuel, born July 5, 1869. Her husband died in 1870. In 1875 she was married to Silas Chamberlain and had these children: Burdine, Dessa, Clarence, Eldon and Julia Ann. Her second husband is dead and she is now a widow for the second time.

Edward Feight, son of Cathrine and grandson of David Smouse, was united in marriage to ———— Acker. To this union three sons were born—Emanuel, William and Calvin.

Julia Ann, daughter of Cathrine and granddaughter of David Smouse, was born January 10, 1827. She was united in marriage to Adam B. Kensinger June 11, 1846. To this union were born five sons and six daughters—John, Isaac, George, Cathrine, Mary, Hannah, Adam, David, Lizzie, Margaret Ann and infant.

John, son of Julia Ann and Adam Kensinger, married Cathrine Helly and had one child, Jennie. Mr. and Mrs. Kensinger are dead.

Jennie Kensinger is united in wedlock to Homer Dilling. Issue: Henry, Paul, Ralph and John.

Isaac, son of Julia Ann and Adam Kensinger, was married to Susan Brumbaugh December 8, 1872. To this union were born the following named children—Elizabeth, Annie, Cathrine, Susie, Adam, Isaac, Margaret, Jeremiah, Minnie, Ellen, Elvin and Grace.

Annie married A. G. Kauffman and has two children— Martha and David.

Cathrine married Aaron Stern and has five children.

Susie married Edward Carper.

Adam married Minnie Quarry and has two children.

Isaac married Mabel Dilling.

George, son of Julia Ann and Adam Kensinger, was united in marriage to Mary Metzker. To this union were born these children—Daniel, Nora, Clara, George, Mary and Cathrine.

Daniel married Amanda Carper. Issue: Philip, George, Mary and infant.

Nora married William Zimmerman. Their children are George, Jacob, Mary, Lester, Grace and Fanny. Lester died very young.

Clara married Albert Carper. They have one son, Lloyd.

Adam married Nancy Ebersole. They have two children.

George and Cathrine are single. Mary is dead. Mrs. George Kensinger suffered for several years with a cancerous tumor, yet amidst all her great pain she was patient and cheerful until the final summons bade her cease to suffer. She closed her eyes in peace with God.

For his second wife Mr. Kensinger married Lizzie Replogle October 22, 1903.

Cathrine, daughter of Julia Ann and Adam Kensinger, was united in marriage to Samuel Metzker. To this union were born four sons—Harry, Adam, Frank and Edward. Mr. and Mrs. Metzker are dead. He was picking apples and fell off of the tree, breaking his neck.

Harry, son of Cathrine and Samuel Metzker, was united in marriage to Sarah Stoner February 16, 1899. To this union were born these children: John S., Cathrine M. and Andrew S.

Adam Metzker is dead.

Frank, son of Cathrine and Samuel Metzker, married Jennie Frederick.

Edward is single.

Mary, daughter of Julia Ann and Adam Kensinger, was married to George Metzker. She is dead. No children were born to this union.

Harriet Kensinger died young.

Lizzie, daughter of Julia Ann and Adam Kensinger, was

united in marriage to Frank Shriver. To this union these children were born: Homer, Anna May, David and Adam.

Adam, David and Margaret Ann, sons and daughter of Julia Ann and Adam Kensinger, are still single.

David, son of David and Mary Smouse, was married to Abigail Hollowell, and these children were born to this union: Nancy, Sophia, Abbie and David.

Nancy, daughter of David and Abigail Smouse, was united in marriage to Paul Smith. To this union were born these children: Mary E., Melda, Eveline, Elmer, Charles, Ida, Edgar, Nellie, Minnie, Scott and Maude.

Mary E., daughter of Paul and Nancy Smith, married J. E. Leach. Their children were Hart and Ella.

Melda, daughter of Paul and Nancy Smith, was united in marriage to S. W. Sullinger. To this union were born Lillie, George, Jennie, Myrtle, Rachael, Homer and Arthur.

Lillie Sullinger married Edward Allbaugh and has three children—Oren, Josie and Samuel.

George Sullinger married ———. Has one child.

Jennie Sullinger married ———. Has one child.

Myrtle Sullinger married ———. Has three children.

Eveline, daughter of Paul and Nancy Smith, married J. W. Noble. To this union were born six children—Clarence, Joseph, Susie, Nannie, Ethel and Coral.

Elmer, son of Paul Smith and Nancy Smith, was united in marriage to Sarah Joslin. To them were born these children: Vera, Howard, Mabel and Garvin E.

Charles, son of Paul and Nancy Smith, was united in marriage to Minnie Wetherel. To this union were born four children—Roy, Ruth, Hazel and William.

Nellie, daughter of Paul and Nancy Smith, married Henry Green. Three children were born to this union—Iva, Edith and Pearl.

Minnie, daughter of Paul and Nancy Smith, married

John Green. To this union were born two sons — Forest and Arthur.

Scott, son of Paul and Nancy Smith, married Oka Cowan. Issue: Josephine, Paul and Ruth.

Sophia, daughter of David and Abigail Smouse, married Beatty Hogue, of Oil City, Pa. Her husband died when only a young man. She was the mother of these children: Garvin, Mame, Willie, Lula, Jennie and Myrtle. Garvin, Jennie and Myrtle are dead. Mame is married, Willie and Lula are single.

Abbie, daughter of David and Abigail Smouse, married Daniel Money. She was the mother of these children: Ida, Arthur, Stephen, Daniel and Mary.

David H., son of David and Abigail Smouse, was married to Elizabeth Thompson, of Glen Hope, Pa. Their children are: Edward, Clark, Alice, Eugene, Wilson, Clare, Lettie, David, Jennie, Guy and Kelia.

Maude Smith, daughter of Nancy and granddaughter of David Smouse, married Wesley Hulbert. No issue.

Barbary, daughter of David and granddaughter of John Smouse, was born June 15, 1810. She was married to John Leonard, and these children were born of this union: Mary J., born December 2, 1833. Jerome, born April 27, 1837. Adam, born July 29, 1838. Elizabeth, born May 18, 1840. John D., born May 18, 1842. Henry N., born December 8, 1843. Rebecca, born July 12, 1845. Jacob S., born July 13, 1847. Cathrine, born October 2, 1849. William, born October 17, 1851, and George F., born January 24, 1854.

The writer was unable to get the data of all the members of the above named children.

Elizabeth, daughter of Barbary (Smouse) Leonard, was born May 18, 1840. She was married to William Ward and had these children — Mary, Lucy, Amanda, Emma, Sarah, John, Ella, George W. and Jacob S.

Mary Ward was united in marriage to Gring Lang and has these children: Lula, Clare, Paul and Fred.

Lucy Ward was born May 4, 1867. She was united in marriage to Benjamin F. Gibbony January 1, 1893. To this union one son was born, Orville, born February 19, 1894.

Amanda Ward married H. D. Russell. Two children are the fruits of this union—Zana and Ruth.

Emma Ward married B. F. Treese. To this union four children were born—Zelda, Ralph, Dewey and Merrill.

Sarah Ward married Alfred Russell. Four children are born to them—Lillian, Arthur, Olive and Homer.

John Ward, son of Elizabeth (Smouse) Ward, married Naomi Lang. To them were born three children—Ida, Benjamin and Martha.

Ella Ward, daughter of Elizabeth (Smouse) Ward, married C. T. Parks. They have two children—Alma and Edna.

George W. Ward married Maggie Foreman and has one child—Harold.

Jacob Sylvester Ward married Phoebe Donelson.

Rebecca, daughter of Barbary (Smouse) Leonard, was united in marriage to William Clouse. To this union were born these children: Elsie, Effie, Edith, Michael, William and Lucy.

Adam, John, Henry, Jacob, George, William, Mary and Cathrine Leonard, children of Barbary (Smouse) Leonard, are all married, but no data was had of their families.

Michael, son of David and grandson of John and Mary Wohlfrom Smouse, was born February 2, 1814 in Snake Spring township, Bedford county, Pa. He remained with his parents on the farm until he was eighteen years of age. He then engaged with Mr. John Miller to learn the blacksmith trade. At the end of two months he left Mr. Miller and the trade and learned the bricklayer's trade, which occupation or trade he followed all his life. He was noted as an able, hon-

est and intelligent workman. He was united in marriage to
Miss Dorothy Loose August 25, 1836. He bought a plot of
ground soon after his marriage, built a log house on the same.
Moved into it in April, 1838, where he raised his family and
where he died March 18, 1875, mourned not only by his
wife and children, but by all who knew him. His was a life
of sunshine and he brought joy and gladness to those with
whom he met. His family consisted of four sons and six
daughters—William H., David F., John L., Mary A., Elizabeth H., Jacob W., Barbary E., Nancy J., Sarah R. and
Maggie M.

William and Sarah Smouse, children of the above named
parents, died in youth.

David F., son of Michael and Dorothy Smouse, was born
December 24, 1839. He was educated in the common schools,
he taught for several years, when in 1871 he entered the employ of the H. & B. T. R. R. as assistant supervisor, which
position he has filled with ability and honor for thirty-five
years. He was married to Pauline Reed for his first wife
and had four children to her—Rosa, George Mc R., Hannah
and infant. For his second wife he married Elizabeth Right-
nour. No children to this union.

George Mc R., son of David F. Smouse, was born May
20, 1870. Married Mary A. Holmes May 21, 1889. To this
union these children were born: Laura E., Charles W., George
F. and Jennie.

Rosa and Hannah are dead.

John L., son of Michael and Dorothy Smouse, was born
January 24, 1841. He was united in marriage to Mary Right-
nour in 1861. His wife and infant died in 1862. In 1863
he married Barbary Burket and to this union was born these
children: William, Nancy, Jacob, David, John C., Jennie,
Cathrine and George. To his third wife he had these children: Harry, John E., Minnie M., Fidella E., Frederick S.

and Nellie E. He was engaged for years as a "Star Route" mail carrier. He died in April 1907 at Marchand, Pa.

William B., son of John L. and grandson of Michael Smouse, was born at Henrietta, Pa., and when quite young left for Claysville, Pa., where he still lives. He is married and has a family, but no data has been obtained.

Nancy, daughter of John L. and granddaughter of Michael Smouse, married Joseph Coy, and to this union were born six children. The writer was unable to get names and dates.

David B., son of John L. and Barbary Smouse, was born at Henrietta, Pa. He entered the employ of the Cambria Iron & Steel Co. when he was but a mere lad. He became an expert in the chemical department, and has held many responsible positions with the C. I. Co., N. Y. S. Co., and is now with the Harrisburg Steel Co. at Harrisburg, Pa., where he has been for ten years. He was united in marriage to Miss Fanny May Weitzell Nov. 16, 1898. Mr. Smouse was born April 4, 1868, and his wife was born October 9, 1876. No issue.

John Calvin, son of John L. and grandson of Michael Smouse, was born at Henrietta, Pa., December 28, 1870. When he was eighteen years old he entered the employ of the Pennsylvania Railroad as locomotive fireman. After several years firing he was promoted, and has been eminently successful as an engineer. He owns a palatial residence at No. 2411 Fourth Ave., Altoona, Pa. He was united in marriage to Miss Vernie Whitesell February 28, 1889. To this union were born these children: Mildred May, October 2, 1890. Dorothy Olive, July 22, 1899.

Cathrine, daughter of John L. and Barbara Smouse, married John Bush. She was the mother of three children when she died. The names are unknown to the writer.

George B., son of John L. and Barbara Smouse, was

born at Henrietta, Pa., June 12, 1872. He has been with the Pennsylvania Railroad as passenger brakeman and conductor for fifteen years. He was united in marriage to Miss Mary Cornelius August 15, 1891. To this union these children were born: Jesse, January 11, 1892. Jennie, February 10, 1894. Nettie, July 10, 1896. Lucy, March 5, 1899.

Jacob, son of John L. and Barbary Smouse, died in infancy.

Jennie, daughter of John L. and Barbary Smouse, was drowned in Johnstown flood. She was a guest of Mrs. Hornick in the Hulburt House when that building in which at the time were three score of occupants, was shattered to atoms by the mighty force of water, almost mountain high.

Minnie, daughter of John L. and Elizabeth Smouse, was born October 30, 1883. She was united in marriage to William Fetterman. To this union were born these children: Bertie, Eugene, Hazel and Harlan.

John E., son of John L. and Elizabeth Smouse, was born May 22, 1881. He was united in wedlock to Emma Sutter, and these children were born of this union: William, Harry and Henry.

Fidella, daughter of John L. and Elizabeth Smouse, was born at Punxsutawney, Pa., August 27, 1886. She married Charles McCulley, a locomotive engineer, of Bellwood, Pa.

Harry, James, Mary, Frederick and Nellie are still at home.

Mary, daughter of Michael and Dorothy Smouse, was born July 9, 1843. She was married to Samuel Burket. She died in December, 1880. Her children were Frederick, Elizabeth, Harry and Laura.

Frederick, son of Mary (Smouse) Burket and grandson of Michael and Dorothy Smouse, was born at Henrietta, Blair county, Pa., December 17, 1862. He served as President of The Smouse Association for five years and was greatly interested in its success. His grandfather, with whom he lived, died March 18, 1875, leaving him at an early age to care for his aged grandmother, which to him was a great pleasure. He was employed by the Pennsylvania Railroad in July, 1881, as a fireman, in which capacity he served for eight years, when he was promoted to be an engineer on the Pittsburg division. He was the engineer of the train which on the evening of December 20, 1897, dashed down the mountain from Gallitzin tunnel at a fearful rate of speed and crashed into a train standing in the yard at the passenger station of Altoona, Pa. The runaway train consisted of forty-five cars drawn by engine 604, which being reversed and running at the rate of a mile a minute, caused the wheels to become red hot. When the engine struck it was lifted like a toy and hurled completely westward. For several minutes the awful grinding continued and then quiet settled on the scene. Locomotives, passenger and freight cars together with poultry and merchandise of all sorts were heaped twenty feet in the air. Marvelous as it may appear the engineer and fireman suffered but slight injuries, though they stood by their posts on the engine while it ploughed into the train ahead, until scarcely a stick of timber or a whole portion of the engine remained. And thus being saved from death, Mr. Burket and the fireman fell upon their knees beside the terrible mass of debris and thanked God for their deliverance. It was no fault of Mr. Burket that the train ran away, and he was exonerated by the Coroner's jury. He was united in marriage to Maude Clark of Utahville, Pa., January 10, 1893, at No. 917 17th street, Altoona, Pa., by the Rev. S. F. Forgeus. To this union were born three children—Dorothy, born February 11, 1895, Daniel Gordon, born November 9, 1896, and Frederick Wooly, born January 30, 1899. He was a member of Calvary Baptist church, the Pennsylvania Railroad relief fund, the Odd Fellows, and the Brotherhood of Locomotive Engineers. He was an active

member of the Pennsylvania Railroad Young Men's Christian
Association and served as Vice President and as a member of
the Board of Directors for a number of years. He died June
3, 1903, after an illness of ten days of typhoid pneumonia.

The following lines of poetry were written in honor of
Mr. Burket:

OUR HEROES OF TO-DAY.

Eighteen hundred, ninety-seven; the twentieth of December
Was a day the people of Altoona will long remember,
'Twas just before Xmas; everything was serene and grand,
And no one dreamed of the dreadful catastrophe so near at hand.

The weather was the dreariest we'd had for many a day,
It rained, snowed and sleeted, while the air was chill and gray,
And people who ventured out you'd hardly think them sane
To see them hurrying with breathless haste to get indoors again.

Far up the mountain on Pennsylvania's famous railroad,
A train was moving along weighed down with a heavy load,
Its speed increased rapidly till it was going at a terrible rate,
And it still kept gaining headway pushed on by its awful weight.

The engineer—brave men who never know or have a fear—
Quickly reversed his engine and tried to stop its mad career:
He whistled help from the train hands, tho' he knew 'twas all in vain,
For a dozen men could not stop the mad rush of that heavy train.

Did he jump and try to save himself? Not that brave engineer.
He thought of all his loved ones and felt that death was near.
Yet he bravely and firmly remained there at his place,
As his train rushed down the mountain at such appalling pace.

He neither looked to the right nor left, but gazed straight on ahead
And saw just then, in its awful distinctness, the danger signal, red.
He pulled the whistle open wide, asked God for His protecting grace;
Reversed his engine once again, and stared Death calmly in the face.

Right before the station, on the same track, he saw another train;
Forgetting not his duty he tried again, with all his might and main,
To slack his speed, but 'twas too late, and with a mighty bound,
They went together with a crash that was heard for a mile around.

The debris and the ruins were almost magnificent in their awfulness,
How great it was only an eye-witness could nearly guess.

They found when it was quiet. after the roar and the tumult,
Three killed and a dozen injured was the sorrowful result.

Three homes where on Xmas would have been happiness and good
    cheer.
Were filled with desolation: were rendered sad and drear.
But that brave engineer was saved! a miracle they say.
Yes, performed by God whom he called on for help that fatal day.

We praise the heroes of the war. and say that they were brave:
Would stand or fall fighting their country's honor to save,
But the heroes of to-day; the men who know no fears:
Who face death every moment. are our noble engineers!

Long live those noble heroes! the men who are true and brave.
Who will always risk their own life some other life to save.
They shirk not their duty, even when death is nigh.
But trust all in their Creator who rules from on high.

LABAN BURKHOLDER

Juniata. January 22. 1898.

Elizabeth Burket, daughter of Mary and granddaughter of Michael and Dorothy Smouse, was born at Henrietta, Pa., January 20, 1870. She was united in marriage to Porter Shultz November 28, 1891. To this union these children were born: Don Bell, August 28, 1892. Paul Frederick, March 1, 1895, died July 14, 1895. Arthur Judson, born June 13, 1896, died January 11, 1897. Alfred Gordon, born August 30, 1898, died March 12, 1900. Samuel Robert, born June 20, 1900, died December 27, 1900, and Mary Elizabeth.

Laura May Burket, daughter of Mary and granddaughter of Michael and Dorothy Smouse, was born at Henrietta, Pa., June 7, 1871. She was united in marriage to George L. Hartman April 3, 1892. To this union the following named children were born: Howard E., born June 9, 1892, died September 24, 1893. Charles Blair, born August 31, 1893. Mary Amelia, born November 18, 1894. Ruth, born July 5, 1896. Edna Elizabeth, born March 20, 1898. Raymond, born ——.

Elizabeth, daughter of Michael and Dorothy Smouse, was born at Henrietta, Pa., November 18, 1845. She was united in marriage to Elias Burket April 28, 1869. The following named children were born to this union: Elmer S., born April 15, 1870. Samuel Clayton, born June 14, 1872, died September 27, 1875. Annie M., born September 27, 1875. Dora S., born September 25, 1878. Nancy Ellen, born August 1, 1881, and Flora S., born December 11, 1883. Mr. Burket died December 7, 1899; his widow married S. S. Nicodemus in 1904.

Elmer S., son of Elizabeth (Smouse) Burket, and grandson of Michael and Dorothy Smouse, was born at Millerstown, Pa., April 15, 1870. He was educated in the schools of North Woodbury township, and early in youth learned the buttermaking trade, at which trade he worked until 1895, when he accepted a position as counter clerk in a wholesale and retail butter store in Altoona, Pa., where he clerked until 1900, when he was offered and accepted the position of traveling salesman for the same firm. At the expiration of one year he resigned his position as salesman to accept the position of shipping clerk in a wholesale grocery house in the same city. One year later he resigned this position and moved with his family to Martinsburg, Pa., where he has been for the past four years in the postal service as a rural carrier He is a prominent member of the orders of the K. G. E. and M. W. of A. He is an officer in the church and a teacher in the Sunday school. He was united in marriage to Harriet Ann Smouse April 20, 1890. To this union are born these children: James Roy, Elias Clark, Elizabeth Rebecca, Lloyd S. Harold Elmer, Flora and Dorothy.

James Roy and Lloyd S. died, the latter in 1897, the first born in 1898.

Annie M., daughter of Elizabeth (Smouse) Burket and granddaughter of Michael and Dorothy Smouse was united in marriage to Simon Stoner July 4, 1894. To this union were born two sons: John S., born September 3, 1894. Lloyd B., born September 30, 1895.

Dora S., daughter of Elizabeth (Smouse) Burket and granddaughter of Michael and Dorothy Smouse, was joined in wedlock to Homer C. Hartman July 28, 1898. These children were born to this union: Elizabeth Amelia, born November 18, 1899, and Helen May, born February 4, 1903.

Nancy Ellen, daughter of Elizabeth (Smouse) Burket and granddaughter of Michael and Dorothy Smouse, was united in marriage to David W. Seedenburg July 10, 1902. To this union were born two daughters—Cathrine Elizabeth, born December 29, 1902, and Grace Cleona, born October 4, 1905.

Flora S., daughter of Elizabeth (Smouse) Burket and granddaughter of Michael and Dorothy Smouse, was united in wedlock to Harry Hyde, of Cumberland, Md. One son was born to this union, Carl Elmer.

John Franklin Hoover, son of Elizabeth and grandson of Michael and Dorothy Smouse, was born November 6, 1867. He was united in marriage to Jennie Anna Howard November 25, 1891. To this union were born these children: Harry Baker Hoover, born August 25, 1892. Flora Glenn Hoover, born May 1, 1894. Gladys May Hoover, born May 18, 1896. John Frederick Hoover, born January 29, 1898, died October 13, 1902. Ella Maria Hoover, born May 30, 1899, died July 15, 1900. Mrs. Jennie A. Hoover was a daughter of L. G. and Flora E. Howard. She was born October 15, 1866, died———

Jacob W., son of Michael and Dorothy Smouse, was born in a log house near Henrietta, Pa., May 20, 1848. He attended the common schools in winter and in summer worked on the farm until he was sixteen years old. Being of a studious disposition he was constantly delving into history, philosophy and mathematics; every spare moment was occupied in gaining an education. He by constant application fitted himself for teaching, and after three terms in the school room as teacher, he entered Greenville Academy and pursued a course of studies to fit himself for the pulpit as well as for the school room. He graduated with honors at the head of his class. Having an ambition in youth to possess a library, he at the age of twelve years commenced its collection, and has been successful in the highest degree, until now he has hundreds of volumes, some of which are rare and costly, having refused one hundred dollars for a German Bible, and also a fabulous price for an ancient Jewish history. He was ordained to the Gospel ministry September 27, 1877. He has been a successful evangelist, adding many hundreds to the church. He was united in the bonds of holy wedlock with Miss Mary Jane Smith, of Smicksburg, Pa., on May 23, 1876. Six children were born to this union—Dorothy Elizabeth, Edgar Monroe, Maggie Eugenie, Edith Viola, Urzulla Devona, and Wilda Elvira.

Dorothy Elizabeth, died aged fifteen years. Urzulla Devona died aged four months.

Edgar M., son of J. W. and M. J. Smouse and grandson of Michael and Dorothy Smouse, was born March 9, 1879. He was united in marriage to Marjorie Zimmerman July 6, 1901. To this union were born these children: Maude Melda, born July 31; 1902, Alton Montelle, born November 14, 1904, and Vernon Lee, born September 26, 1906.

M. Eugenie, daughter of J. W. and M. J. Smouse and granddaughter of Michael and Dorothy Smouse, was born October 10, 1881. She was united in marriage to Webster J. Colbert March 22, 1905. Two children were born to this union: Charles Warren, born October 11, 1905, and Chester Edgar, born August 7, 1907.

Edith V., daughter of J. W. and M. J. Smouse and granddaughter of Michael and Dorothy Smouse, was born November 22, 1884. She was united in marriage to David B. Stoudnour November 28, 1907. One son was born to this union: Lemmon Clare.

Wilda E. daughter of J. W. and M. J. Smouse and grand daughter of Michael and Dorothy Smouse, was born March 18, 1891. She is still in school.

Barbary E., daughter of Michael and Dorothy Smouse, was born October 5, 1850. On December 22, 1872, she was married to John H. Coy of Saxton, Pa. The ceremony was performed by J. L. Dougherty. Five children were born to this union—Charles H., born August 23, 1873, died April 13, 1874. Susan E., born November 15, 1875, died January 13, 1876. W. Harvey, born September 6, 1880, died October 2, 1880. Infant daughter born November 6, 1886—dead. Merrill C., born April 2, 1895. Mr. Coy died very suddenly at his work July 24, 1898. Mrs Coy lives in her own home at Saxton, Pa.

Nancy, daughter of Michael and Dorothy Smouse, was born November 9, 1852. She was united in marriage to Moses B. Stonerook of Henrietta, Pa. Three sons, Daniel, James and Charles, were born to this union. Daniel died quite young.

Maggie, daughter of Michael and Dorothy Smouse, was born November 17, 1858. She was married to John Stewart. Her children were Edward, Robert, Henry, Dora and David. She died in May, 1899, at Punxsutawney, Pa., and was buried in Fair Hope Cemetery.

Nancy, daughter of David and granddaughter of John and Mary Smouse, was born near Everett, Pa. She was united in marriage to Solomon Koontz, of Bedford, Pa. They emigrated to Athens county, Ohio, when it was yet a wilderness. No children to bless them. Mr. and Mrs. Koontz are both dead.

Eve, daughter of David and granddaughter of John and Mary Smouse, was born near Everett, Pa. She married George Defibaugh, a brother to John and William. These two located near Chaneysville, Pa., where they raised a family of children. The writer was unable to get any data as to their children. Mrs. Defibaugh died in 1869.

Frederick, son of David and grandson of John and Mary Smouse, was the youngest child. He died when fourteen years of age and is the only one of the family buried in the cemetery with his parents.

Jennie F. Newman, daughter of John Thomas and great granddaughter of Peter Smouse and her brother Ramey Thomas, were left orphans, she at three weeks of age and her brother at three years of age. Her brother died a few years ago. She was left a widow with three children, who are now in prospering circumstances. She is in her fifty-third year, and is in business at 647 West Franklin street, Baltimore, Maryland.

Reid S. Shipley, 3005 Matthews Avenue, (Waverly) Baltimore, Maryland, is a grandson of Abraham and Louisa (Smouse) Haldeman. His grand uncles are William and Edward Smouse, of Oakland, and Daniel and Henry Smouse of Grantsville, Maryland. The author has been unable to get any data from the family save this brief sketch of Mr. Reid S. Shipley.

Henry Smouse, a brother of John, located in Frederick county, Maryland. The writer has no data of his family except that given in Isenberg History by the Rev. J. M. S. Isenberg, and the author of this work is greatly indebted to Rev. Isenberg for so freely assisting in furnishing data, and in giving a brief biography of himself.

The following history of the three daughters of Mr. Smouse who married into the Isenberg family is taken verbatim from Isenberg History—

Enoch, Nicholas and Peter married sisters, daughters of one Henry Smouse. Enoch married Dorothy Smouse, born November 28, 1764. Nicholas married Mary and Peter married Margaret. (The Smouse family Bible, brought from Maryland to Pennsylvania, is in the writer's possession, a precious heirloom. The records of the same, except a fragment, have been lost, it having been rebound early in this century.) No record has been found of the maiden name of Henry's wife.

Enoch Isenberg's Descendants.

NOTE —To economize, the following abbreviations have been used:
d. for dead, m. for married. The name of the State of residence is
given only when such State is other than Pennsylvania. The ad-
dresses are given where known. Of course, the address of the children of the present generation is the same as that of parents unless
otherwise indicated.

1. George (1785-1829), m., 1810, Nancy Wise, Barree.
    1. John Enoch (1813–1865), m., 1839, Barbara A.
        Wolheater, d.
        1. Clifford A. (1847-), m., 1872, Kate M. Smith,
            Alexandria.
                Sarah A., Harry C., James H., Maud M.,
                Ethel M., Bula J., Ruth M., John
                W., Lottie K.
        2. George W. (1849-) a bachelor, 34 Reg. Co. I,
            June, 1861, wounded May 29, 1864,
            Alexandria.
        3. Theodore F., (1851-), m ————, Henderson
            Township, Huntingdon County.
            Ella, d., several other children.
        4. Mary F. (1853-), m., 1874, James G. Murphy,
            Orbisonia.
                Alexander S., Malissa B., Mary A., Charles
                W., Annie E., James A., Hannah M.
        5. Annie E. (1855-), m., 1889, L. Gemmill Cress-
            well, Petersburg.
                Beulah, Mary Gemmill, Robert N. and
                Henry C.

6. Malissa K. (1858-1891), m., 1883, Henry Sellers. Orbisonia.

Laurence, Myrtle May, Neuville N.

7. Michael G., (1859), m., 1897, Annie Paine (1860), Philadelphia.

George W.

2. Daniel (1815-1893), m., 1842, Caroline Taxis.

1. Annie P. (1843), m. 1866, John T. Lucas, Moshannon.

Edith L., Harry D.

Cyrus C., m., 1895, Minnie Edmond.

Miriam S.

Carrie E., John T., James W., Clarence T.

Anna I., Miriam P., Jennie M., Albert C.

3. Henry, d 1837, at 20.

4. Michael W., m Susanna Wolheater, both d.

1. Mary, d. in infancy.

2. George W., (1844), m 1865, Nancy Geesey, Marshalltown, Iowa.

Ray.

Perry, d in infancy.

Ellie, m W. K. Baird.

One child.

Susan, m Longman.

Two children.

Margaret, Hays, Frank, Ray.

3. Albert, d in infancy.

4. Charles T., d when a young man.

5. Sarah, maiden lady.

6. Joseph, d in infancy.

7. Susan, maiden lady, California.

8. Maria L., m D. H. Carles, Altoona.

Frank, Jessie, d, Chester, Mary, d. Ralph, Rilla.

9. Blair, m Clara J. Baird, Frankstown,
   C. Roy, Elda.

10. John A., m Annie L. Stultz.
    Susan P., Rhoda C., Daniel S.
    Blair A.

5. Mary Ann, (1825–1887), m 1842.

First husband, Alexander Work, d.

1. Margaret A., m 1867, Wm.
   C. Goodwin, Rock Springs.
   Mary A., m —— Weber.
   Margery, Nancy J., Wm. C.,
   Henry S. M.

Second husband, Peter Grabill, d.
One child, d.
Third husband, m 1855, Dan Fet-
terhoof, d 1863.
Fourth husband, m 1873, John
Shall, d 1886.

II. Henry (1787–1869), m Elizabeth Caracker, d 1857, lived
near Alexandria, subsequently McConnellstown.

1. Samuel (1816–88), m Maria Brown, d.
   Known as Big Sam.

2. George, d young.

3. Eve, d young.

4. Henry m 1840, Elizabeth Hamer, lived at Mc-
   Connellstown, latter days, both d.

1. Alfred P., m 1866, P. A. Barnett, Superintend-
   ant of mines, Beccaria.
   George B., m Jennie Wagner, Ramey.
   four children.
   J. Henry, m Dora Smith, Pittsburg.
   Four children.
   Bertha O., m Frank Brown d.
   Two children.

Vinetta A., m Rev. S. F. Rounsley, M. E.
minister, Trout Run.

Anna May, m Rev. J. E. Allgood, M. P.
minister, Lickingsville.

Two children.

Samuel B., m Annie Boon, Osceola.

One child.

Linda A., A. Percy, Charles W., Wm. H.
D. Bruce, Ferda at home.

Robert P. and Edgar, d in infancy.

2. George W., 125th Reg. Pa. Vol., Co. C., d 1862.

3. Jennie, m 1871, John Wighaman, Punxsutawney.
Harry N., adopted son.

4. Mary, m George Bradley, Broad Top City.

Wm. m Annie Mears, Broad Top City.

Three children.

Ella, m Morgan, Tyrone.

Two children.

Amy, John, Catharine, Carrie, Annie, George.

5. Susan, m 1873, C. Z. Zimmerman, Altoona.

Corwin, m Catharine Morain, Altoona.

Irene.

Mary.

6. Juniata, m 1888, H. C. Powley, Houtzdale.

Howard C., Dorothy M.

5. Daniel, m twice, d 1889, Shirleysburg. Four sons killed.

First wife, Susannah Foster, d.

1. James, killed in battle of Antietam.

2. Henry, killed by tree falling on him.

3. Samuel, killed by wagon running over him.

4. Cathrine, m 1865, Abram Wicks, Cyclone.

Ira B., and Myrtle B.

5. Joseph P., m 1875, Mary E. Glass, Bradwick.

G. Allen, Flora E., Elsie M. and Fannie G.

6.   Lewis, m Flora Glass, Olean, N. Y.
      Charles.

Second wife, Susannah Sanders, still living.

7.   Enoch, m Alice Parsons, Aughwick Mills.
      Grace and Mary.

8.   Lizzie, m Wm. Green, Altoona.
        Nellie, Clifford, George, two children d.

9.   George, m Mintie Hooper, killed in P R R yard
      Altoona.
        Otto, Hellen, Ray, Erwin.

10.   Nancy, m Oliver Smith, Birmingham.
        Hellen, Charles D., Susan E., Sadie.

11.   William died when a young man.

6.   Joseph (1825), married twice, McConnellstown.

First wife, 1852, Mary Hamer, d 1853.
      Samuel Reid, d.

Second wife, 1859, Mary Ann Norris (1830).

1.   Lizzie May, (1862), m 1891, C. Rufus McCarthy.
      Huntingdon.

The record of the family of Mrs. C. R. McCarthy from
1761, or earlier, don't know date previous.

John Henry Isenberg lived in Maryland.

Enoch, second son, born April 4, 1761, came to Pennsylvania in 1802, married Dorothy Smouse, born November 28,
1764, daughter of Henry Smouse, and lived near Alexandria
on the farm now known as the Robert Laird farm, which he
then owned.

Henry, second son of Enoch, was born 1787, died 1869.
Married Elizabeth Caraher, (or spelled Caracker, I think the
first is correct), who died 1857.   Lived near Alexandria, later
near McConnellstown.

Joseph, sixth child of Henry, was born 1825, died 1902.
Married twice; lived in McConnellstown.

I will quote a few remarks made by Rev. M. H. Sangree,
D. D., of Harrisburg, Pa., in his memoriam of father, who
knew him from a boy until death:

"His life by inheritance and early training was built of
heroic material. He was not an ordinary boy, amid the
many temptations and attempts to lead him away. He re-
vered God, honored the Sabbath, read his Bible, went to church,
searched for good books, sought the companionship of good
men; he was industrious, exact and honest. This was his
young manhood, as I remember it. And these marks of his
early life continued through his maturer years and made it
what it was, a very noble life. He was an honored elder in
the Reformed church from early manhood."

First wife m 1852, Mary Hamer, d 1853.

Samuel Reid Isenberg died ———

Second wife m 1859, Mary A. Norris, born 1830, daughter of Joseph Norris, near Grafton, Pa.

Lizzie May Isenberg, born 1862, married 1891, C. Rufus
McCarthy, merchant of Huntingdon, Pa.

John Donald McCarthy, born 1894.

Ruth born 1897, died same year.

Harry Isenberg born 1900.

    2.   Warren D., (1864), m 1890, Fannie Weir,
           Lawyer, St. Louis, Mo.
           Mary Frank, Joseph Warren, Robert Weir.

    3.   Joseph Kieffer, (1866), m 1887, Maggie Hicks,
           Altoona.
           A. Roy and a baby boy.

    4.   James Milton Sangree, (1871), m 1896, Mary E.
           Heffner, (1871), Reformed minister, Trinity
           church, Philadelphia.

James Milton Sangree, son of Joseph Isenberg and Mary
Ann Norris, was born at McConnellstown, Pa., January 1,
1871. He was baptized in infancy and after a confession of

faith in our Lord Jesus Christ was confirmed in Trinity Reformed church of that place at the age of sixteen.

His early education was obtained in the public schools of that town. At the age of seventeen he entered Ursinus Academy at Collegeville, Pa. He was graduated from Ursinus College with high honors in 1893. Three years later he was graduated from the School of Theology then at that place, being awarded the two prizes offered in Church History.

He was licensed to preach the gospel by Juniata Classis of the Reformed church in annual session at Marklesburg, Pa., 1896. He was then called to the pastorate of the Durham Reformed charge, Durham, Pa., where he was ordained to the Christian ministry. His pastorate at this point covered a period of sixteen months, when he resigned October 1, 1897, to accept a call to the First Reformed church, Spring City, Pa. This pastorate covered a period of seven years and a half. He resigned this pastorate to accept a call to Trinity Reformed church, Philadelphia. He began his pastorate in Philadelphia, February 1, 1905.

Splendid success has crowned his labors in each of these fields of labor. His present pastorate is in one of the first churches of the denomination, distinguished alike for its aggressive work and large benevolent contributions.

He has been honored by election to a number of positions of trust and responsibility. He is one of the managers of Pennsylvania Bible Society, the oldest Bible society in America. He is a Director of his Alma Mater, Ursinus College, having been elected to this office by his fellow alumni. He is also a member of the Board of Visitors to the Central Theological Seminary, Dayton, Ohio.

In May, 1896, he was united in marriage with Mary Heffner, of McConnellstown, Pa. Three children have blessed this union—Paul Heffner, aged 10 years; Lillian Marie, aged 6 years; and Helen Frances, aged 5 years.

He has been the historian of the Isenberg family, whose ancestry has been so closely related to that of the Smouses. He is now engaged on a new and enlarged history of the family. His present home address is 1541 N 7th street, Philadelphia.

7. Dorothy, d 1897, m J. W. Yocum (1826), Raystown Branch, Huntingdon county.
   1. Alonzo B., 1853, a bachelor.
   2. Clarence P., died in infancy.
   3. James Alvin, (1856) m ———
      Two children.
   4. Silas Henry, (1858)
   5. Lizzie Maggie, (1860)
   6. Horatio G. F. (1862), m Ada N. White.
      Dorothy M., John W., Martha L.
   7. Martha H., (1866), m 1888, W. B. White.
      Carey E., Anna W., and baby boy.
   8. Mary M., (1869), m 1895, Irwin Leibensperger, Huntingdon.
      Alva L., Joseph Y.

III. Daniel, (1789) m Leffard, both dead.
   1. Anna, m 1840 Nathan Lafferty, Kipple, Blair county.
      1. Margaret, d.
      2. Amanda, m 1860 Adam Vanallman.
         Wm. Dorthula, John, Daniel, Annie, Clara. Irene, Joseph, Ida and Alice.
      3. Wm. d.
      4. Mary, m 1874, J. A. Booher.
         Flora, Marilla, Charles, Dorris, George, Anna, Bell, Nora Maud, Gertrude.
      5. Daniel, m 1880, Eliza J. Taneyhill.
      6. Clara J., m 1875, Blair Moore.
         Harry, Isabella, Ida, Cora, and Elsie, d, Viola, Bertha, Charles.

7. Ida, m 1885, Samuel C. Bressler.
   Annie, Bertha, Cora, Minnie, John C.
8. Emma, m 1883, Howard Sharp.
   Annie, Elmer, Clarence, Earl, Cora, Roy.

2. Margaret m 1848, James Smith, Orbisonia.
   1. Isabelle, m William Daughenbaugh, Rock Hill.
   2. John L., Chicago, Ill.
   3. Catharine, m William Hewitt Isenberg.
      For children, see William of Nicholas.
   4. Daniel I., of Orbisonia.
   5. Annie M., m George Miller, Marietta, Ohio.
      Four boys.
   6. William B., Marietta, Ohio.
   7. George B. McClelland, Marietta, Ohio.

3. William L., m Rebecca Hughes, McConnellstown.
   1. Samuel H., m 1881, Etta J. Irvine, minister,
      Millersburg.
      G. Carl and Ethel I.
   2. John L., m 1877, Elizabeth Hamer, McConnells-
      town.
      Harry H., m 1900, Mary Fraker.
      Frank W., Charles L.
   3. David L., m 1879, Martha Isenberg, Alexandria.
      Malvin B., Newton H., Rhoda, two children
      dead.
   4. D. Alice, m 1877, S. B. Stouffer, Alexandria.
      Ida, m Edward Helyer.
      Mary Alice.
      W. Cloyd, M. Myrtle.
   5. W. Frank, m 1892, Carrie H. Long, Professor,
      Altoona.
      Irvin H.
   6. Laura, m 1894, William Stouffer, Altoona.
      J. Clair, W. Charles.

4. Enoch, d
5. Ansavilla, d
6. Catharine, d
7. Emily, m Wolfe, Altoona.
    1. Lewis
    2. Catharine
    3. Calvin
    4. Annie
    5. Laura
    6. Walter
    7. Ross
    8. Harrison
8. John C., m Mary Ann Heffner, contractor, Hunting
        don.
    1. Virginia, d
    2. Jennie, d m John Miller.
            Two children
    3. Harry d
    4. Lorilla, m John Miller.
    5. Orladay, m Annie Barrick.
            Margaret.
    6. Carrie, m William Wilson, grandson of Anna Mary
                (Isenberg) Hoffman.
            Son and daughter.
    7. Maggie, m Dr. Schofield, Shirleysburg.
            Two children.
    8. Ray, m ———
9. Daniel, m Shaffer, Altoona.
10. Isabelle m 1863, Peter Piper, Alexandria.
    1. Jesse B., m 1887, B. Alice Barr, Pine Grove Mills.
            Belle Florence, Anna Margaret.
    2. William R.
    3. Joseph M.
    4. Bertha M., m 1898, Charles A. Spyker.
            Harold L.

IV. Catharine (1791 d), Samuel Grove, lived near Orbisonia.

  1. Joseph, d m Martha Colgate, d McConnellstown.

    1. Lizzie, m David Isenberg, Orbisonia.
       Bertha, m George Hoover, Grafton.
       John.

    2. Malinda, m David Kurtz, Shirleysburg.
       Luden, Rell, m ———, Pittsburg.
       Alverta, (Annie and Isabel d) Joseph, Leona.
       William.

    3. Annie, m Calvin Enyeart.
       James, Myrtle, Calvin Zwingli, Arthur.

    4. Samuel, m Malissa McMullen, Saltillo.
       Louisa, m Green.
       Ella, several more girls.

    5. Martha, d m William Heffner, McConnellstown.
       Ella L., m Bunn Johnson.
         Donald Scott.
       Maud, d
       Pearl G.

    6. James, first wife, Maggie Harris, d
       Boy.
       Second wife, Mary Johns.

    7. Joseph M., m Sarah Harris, Canton, Ohio.
       Calvin, Alda, Martha, Blanche, May, Emman-
       uel, Binkley, two boys.

  2. Dorothy, maiden lady, d

  3. John, d m Mary Miller, d Shirleysburg.

    1. Joseph, m Nancy Harris.

    2. Martha, m M. K. Hamer, McConnellstown.
       Minerva, m Sam Moyer.
       Kate, m George Kobb.
         Two children.
       Scott, m Clara Fraker, Huntingdon.

John, m Gertrude Bupp, Altoona.

Marie and Martha.

Mary, m 1899, Irwin Coulter.

Marshall, Lydia, Ella, Sarah, Retta.

3. David, first wife, Lucretia Megahan, d
   Three children.

   Second wife, Caroline Ambrose.

   Several children.

4. Jackson L., m Naomi Isenberg.
   Ruth, Howard, Florence, Mahlon, Elizabeth,
   Alma, Lawrence, Emma.

5. Catharine, m Solomon H. Grove.

6. Samuel H., d at 13.

4. Susannah, m John Enyeart, Shirleysburg.

   1. Kate, m John Harvey.

   2. D. P., m Sarah Daniels.

   3. Dorothy, m John Grove.

   4. Maggie, m A. J. Kelley.

   5. Lizzie.

   6. Samuel,)
   7. George,   } died young.
   8. Sarah,   )

5. Solomon, m Jane Huntzman.

   1. William, m Isabella Bolinger.

   2. John, m Dorothy Enyeart.

   3. Dorothy, m Jacob Hatt.

   4. Alice, m Elmer Miller.

   5. Bruce, m Annie Doyle.

   6. Harry.

   7. Catharine, m Harvey Gettig.

   8. George, m Nettie Rutter.

   9. Mary.

   10. Abraham,)
   11. Lewis,   } died young.
   12. Ellen,   )

6. David, m Martha Price, Orbisonia.

  1. Enoch, first wife, Annie Trexler, d
    Second wife, Jane Giles.

  2. Annie.

  3. George, m Nancy Sechrist.

  4. Frank, m Annie Tonnyhill.

  5. Harriet, m Estella Collins.

  6. Roy.

7. Samuel, m Mary Foster.

  1. Solomon H., m Kate Grove.

  2. Kate.

  3. Henry.

  4. Baby, dead.

8. Kate, m William Rutter, Waterloo, Iowa.

  1. Emma.

  2. Cora.

  3. Harry.

  4. Franklin.

  5. Edward.

  6. Samuel.

9. Abram, m Kate Hammond.

  1. Samuel, m Malissa Sechrist.

  2. Belle, m Monroe Sechrist.

  3. Clara, m George Long.

  4. Maggie, m William Sechrist.

  5. Dorothy, m Luther Sechrist.

  6. Oliver, } died young.
  7. Enoch, }

V. Susannah (1793 d), m Philip Piper, Alexandria.

1. John, Altoona.

2. Joseph, m Julia Ann Piper, of Ann Margaret Isenberg of Nicholas. See children under his family.

3. Enoch.

4. Philip.

5. Abraham.
6. William.
7. Lydia, m ——— Piper.
8. Polly, m ——— Walker.
9. Maggie, m Henry Graffius.

VI. Joseph (1775–1880), m Elizabeth Piper, d 1866. Canoe
Valley, Blair County.

1. Dorothy, d 1848, m 1846, William of Benjamin, of
Nicholas.

  1. Drucilla, d

2 John, (1824) m 1850 Mary Kimberling, Cove Forge

  1. Robert S., m 1881, Amanda E. Bridenthal, merchant, Woodbury, Bedford county.

    Emerson, ⎫
    Bruce,   ⎬ were twins, Bruce d

  2. Joseph, m Christiana Stewart.

    John S., Ella, Maud, Mary M., Susan U.,
William M.

  3. Thornton B., m 1874, Keturah A. Mountz, Martinsburg.

    Charles E., Wheeler L., Alice K., Cora M.

  4. Walter, m Clara Dell, d

    Blair E., Minnie B., Carrie C.

  5. Lewis H., m Martha J. Bacon.

    Lola C., Annie C., Albert S., Edna L., Mary
S., Bertha I.

  6. Lucy M., m Stewart Brantner.

    Seymour P.

  7. Minnie B.

  8. Seymour M., m Annie L. Potter.

    Ralph W.

  9. Albert, m Nancy Rhodes.

    Orville J., Ellie C., Millard C.

  10. Alice K.

3. Enoch, m 1863, Catharine Shaffer, Yellow Springs.
  1. Lizzie, m 1892, F. L. Black, Pine Grove Mills.
        Freda A., Ethel M., Mildred A., Norman E.
  2. Calvin B.
  3. Porter G., m 1891, Caroline Schirm.
  4. Asa C.
  5. Dorothy.
  6. Ella.
  7. Grace.
  8. Lynn S.
  9. Blanche.
4. George, died young.
5. Catharine, maiden lady, Yellow Springs.
6. Margaret, m 1861, David Heilman, Water Street.
  1. Ida D., m 1884, Josiah Harnish.
        Lynn H., Clair L., Arthur E., Alton Roy.
  2. Della Irene.
  3. Bertha K., m 1886, Arthur M. Roller.
        Walter R., Minerva J., Howard, Vinona G.
  4. Lizzie G., d
  5. Mary B., d
  6. Dessa May.
  7. Walter Scott.
  8. Uton Lloyd.
  9. Cecilia J., d
7. Clara, d 1877, m 1869, James F. Carothers, Danville, Va.
  1. Annie.
  2. Celia, d at 19.
  3. Joseph, Jacksonville, Fla.
VII. Abram (1798–1884), m 1821, Nancy Grove (1806–75), Cross Roads.
  1. Susannah (1823) m John Metz. Both d, Williamsburg.

1. Thomas J. Metz, m Jennie Patton.
   Two children.
2. Ann Dorothy, m John Frank.
   Six children.
3. Catharine E., m Joseph Orlady, both d
   Tacy R., m R. R. Roller.
   Katherine.
4. Abraham Ross, m 1877, Hannah Bennett, merchant, Philadelphia.
   Elwood Paul, John Clifford.
5. Cecil Spaner, died young.
6 John Grove, m Julia Patterson.
   J. Alfred, Ray, Harry.
7. Joseph Stewart, ⎰
8. Calvin More, ⎰ merchants, Williamsburg.
9. Lettie, m James Smith, d
   Nannie Kathleen.

2. Thomas, (1824-82), m 1855, Mary W. Fox, Graysville, Huntingdon county.
   1. Anna Kate (1857), m 1874, John Bateman, Bris-
      bin.
      Thomas Howard (1875), m Catharine Evans.
      Russel Guy, Robert Earl,
      Lillie May (1879).
   2. Susan Viola, m 1883, J. H. Beck, McVeytown.
      Ralph and Mary E, both d
   3. Harry Grove, (1861), m Alice Whipple, Lewistown.
      Bertha, William and Charles, twins.
   4. Lillie May (1862), m Samuel Frank, Graysville.
      Lloyd.
   5. John W., d
   6. Mary Isett (1866), m William Carter, Olean
      New York.
      Harry, d, Pearl.

7. Rebecca Jane (1866), twin sister to Mary, m
   1884, Thomas Lloyd (1863), Brisbin.
   Edna May (1885), Delia (1893), Leslie Clare,
   (1898).

8. Abigail Lloyd (1868), m William Farber, Benore.
   Leroy, Grace, Paul and Ruth, twins.

9. Charles A. (1871), m Della Shutt, Bradford.
   Edward, Charles and Gertrude, twins, d

10. Edward (1874).

11. Gertrude E. (1877), m 1899, Edward Wetherson,
    Brisbin.

12. John C (1881).

3. Catharine (1827), m 1852, William Johnston (1827),
   Altoona.

   1. Thomas F (1853), m 1873, Martha A. Champeno
      (1842).
      Agnes Boulten (1879).
      Catharine Elizabeth (1881).

   2. Samuel R. (1855-56).

   3. Lewis C. (1856), m 1890, Margaret A. Donahue
      (1856).
      Catharine Dorothy, (1893).

   4. John M. (1859), m 1888, first wife Nettie R. Am-
      hiser (1867 90).
      George William, (1889).
      John Reese, d 1890.
      Second wife, 1897, Sarah Margaret Stonebraker
      (1870).

   5. Ada Jane (1860), m 1879, Cassius M. Johnson.
      William Ira, George Roy, Cassius E., d, Ray-
      mond M., Ada G., Lewis M., Hellen R

   6. Nancy Grove (1862).

   7. Margaret Ann (1864).

   8. Susannah D. (1867).

9. Mary C. (1870–72).

4. Dorothy (1828), m 1857, Enoch Walls, Hollidaysburg.

 1. Susannah M. (1858), m 1875, William Van All-
man, Roaring Spring.

  Lola Dorothy (1876).

  Emma Brunette (1878).

  Irene Catharine (1880).

 2. Nancy C. (1859), m J. T. Rodkey.

  Harry E., Edward L., Nellie G., John L., d

 3. Carrie P. (1861–64).

 4. William F. (1863). Kate Keller. Ehrenfeld.

 5. Jacob M. (1865), m 1887, Delia Clapper.

  Carrie R., Velva P.

 6. Lizzie S. (1868), m 1890, James Edmund Stewart, Altoona.

  Otho Verner.

5. Jacob Miller (1831), m 1856, Susannah Wolford,
Jacksonville, Florida.

 1. A. Rupley (1857), m 1878, Maggie J. Shultzabar-
ger, Altoona.

  M. Edna, Ethel B., G. Fred., Bruce M.

 2. Annie E. (1858), m 1881, J. B. Shoenfelt, Musco-
gee, Indian Territory.

  Hattie Pearl, Cecil Earl, Doris Edna.

 3. John W. (1859), Johnstown, musician.

 4. Lucy E. (1861), m 1881, D. A. Stewart, Iron
Mountain, Michigan.

  Grace R., Dora Isabel.

 5. Herbert, (1866), m 1888, Alice M. Gunnett,
Johnstown.

  Charlotte V., Cloyd W., Edith O.

 6. Ralph B. (1873).

6. Solomon H. (1834), m 1859, Adaline R. Stewart

(1841), merchant, Altoona.

1. Charles H. (1860), m 1884, Annie Grove, Chambersburg.
   Blair F., Mary G.

2. Harry M. (1862), m 1884, Ida Johnson, Pottsville.
   S. Lloyd, Clifford E., d, Ruth M.

3. Alvin M., (1863-80).

4. Abram F. (1866-74).

5. Joseph L. (1868), m 1894, Ella M, Homer, physician, Mines.
   Kathleen H. and Hobart C., d, Howard Clair.

6. Jennie (1870).

7. Bruce R. (1873-77).

8. Elsie Kate (1875).

9. Mattie Boyer (1877), m 1898, M. E. Treese.

10. Grettie Smith (1879).

7. Joseph Grove (1836), m Lucretia Duffy 1844, lawyer, ex-sheriff, ex-judge, merchant, Huntingdon.

   1. Frank B. (1870.)

   2. Lenore (1872), m 1899, James Woods, Esq., Huntingdon.

8. John Harnish (1838-50).

9. Samuel B. (1841), m 1862, Caroline Swope (1843-98), Tyrone, salesman. Miller by trade, Superintendent of iron ore mines and quarries up to '95. Two terms in Pennsylvania Legislature.

   1. Essington S. (1863), m 1875, Jane M. McCamant, California.
      Helen C., Elizabeth M., Walter E., Samuel H., Mary M.

98

2. James C. (1865), m 1890, Laura L. Nepper, merchant, Williamsburg.
   Karl S., Hilda S., Wayne N., Frank R.
3. Crawford I. (1867), m 1892, Maggie Benton, Birmingham.
   Everett P., Albert A., Daniel R., baby.
4. Clara B. (1866), m 1890, Albert Hovarter, Chicago.
   Clyde G., Ruth A., Bell, m
5. Fannie M. (1871), m 1896, H. C. Madison, Pittsburg.
   Caroline L., Richard.
6. Mary S. (1873), m 1895, E. H. Faulkender, Esq., Hollidaysburg.
   Ruth I.
7. Lucy E. (1875), m 1899, G. E. Brehman, Altoona.
8. Carrie R. (1879-80).
9. Daisie G. (1882).
10. Jessie C. (1885).
11. Paul P. (1889).

10. B. Frank (1844), m 1869, Jennie McCahan, head
    of Milling Company, President Pennsylvania
    State Millers' Insurance Company, Huntingdon, Pa.
    1. Frank M., m Belle Letterman, Huntingdon.
       Benj. Franklin.
    2. Jesse M., Wilmerding.

VIII. Samuel, never married, died at 45, while other ten of
       family, all of whom married, lived to be over
       80 years.
IX. Anna (1799d), m Cross, d, Alexandria.
    1. Benj., d, m ——— Saner, Alexandria.
       1. Andrew, m ———, Hollidaysburg.
       2. Charles, m ———, Indianapolis.

  3. Annie, m Bowers, Altoona.

  4. Ida, m William Gerst, Altoona.

    Fred, Mary, Hellen.

 2. Mary, m Gross.

X. Anna Mary (Aunt Polly) (1801-98), m 1828, Jacob Hoffman, Alexandria.

  1. Catharine, d

  2. William, d

  3. Anna Rebecca, m John Rough, d, Altoona.

    1. George.

    2. Bertha M., d

    3. James, d

    4. Annie.

    5. Ida.

  4. Mary, m David Wilson, Huntingdon.

    1. William, m Carrie Isenberg, granddaughter of Daniel of Enoch.

  5. Susan, m 1863, Nicholas Piper.

    1. Carrie Ann.

    2. M. Salome, m William Spyker, d

    3. Ella M.

    4. Bessie M.

  6. Peter, d.

  7. Henry A., m 1863, Martha M. Snyder, Tyrone.

    1. William E., m 1894, Iole J. McEwen.

      William E. and John M.

    2. John S., m 1893, Eleanor Hewitt.

      Harry H. and Eleanor J.

    3. Mary Ellie, d

    4. Henry Wood, d

    5. Sallie Stewart, m 1891, William W. Locke.

      Raymond B., d

      Milton I., d

    6. Catharine Salome.

7. Addie Susan.
8. Edith Walton.
9. Milton Duncan.

8. Jacob A., m 1870, Clarissa Wilson, Tyrone.
  1. M. Aida.
  2. Charles L., m Annie L. Hart.
     C. Allen, Richard J., C. Fessler.
  3. S. Augusta.
  4. Grace W.
  5. Walter H.
  6. A. Gertrude.
  7. W. Claire.
9. Wilhelmina, maiden lady, Alexandria.
  Two children died in infancy.

XI. Enoch (1804 d), m Lefford, d, Alexandria.
  1. Anna Catharine, maiden lady.
  2. Anna Mary, m Benjamin Isenberg of William of Nicholas.
    For children see under same.
  3. Jacob, m Sarah Isenberg of William of Nicholas, Alexandria.
    1. Elwood M.
    2. Alfred G.
    3. William V.
    4. Salome, m Ammerman, Tyrone.
    5. Jennie, m Stair, Altoona.
    6. Alice, m Wallace, Altoona.
    7. Benjamin C.
    8. Mahlon P.
    9. Webster B.
  4. Susan, d young.
  5. William H., m twice, Alexandria.
    First wife, Tamar Folk.
    Son, m

Three daughters, all m

Second wife, Kate ———.

Daughter.

6. Annsavilla, d 1885, m 1866, Silas W. Isenberg of
     Nicholas of Benjamin of Nicholas.
     For children see under same.

7. Samuel V., m 1865, Elizabeth A. Garland, Tacoma,
     Washington, Company C., 125th Regiment
     Pennsylvania Vol.

    1. Letitia Melissa, m 1889, Charles P. Sharman.
        Samuel and Charles.

    2. Walter Scott, m 1896, Lila McMullen.
        Walter John and Lester Samuel.

    3. Jennetta May.

    4. Joseph Curtin.

8. B. R., m Mary C. Parker, McKeesport.

    1. Rogena, m Foster.

    2. Lizzie, m Bailey.

    3. Levina.

    4. Lottie, m Prosser.

    5. William.

    6. Emma, m Selway.

    7. David L., an evangelist.

    8. Mary, d.

    9. Carrie, m Pollock.

    10. Samuel.

    11. Hugh.

    12. Eugene, d

    13. Charles.

    14. Lillie B., d

Descendants of Nicholas Isenberg

I. John, d, m 1823, Mary Piper, d
  1. Samuel, d in Ohio, never married.
  2. Ephraim, d in Kansas, never married.
  3. John, d at 14.
  4. Susannah, d, never married.
  5. Julia Ann, d, never married.
  6. Anna Mary, m Veach.
      One child. } All dead.

II. Enoch, m Sarah Caldwell, no children, both d

III. Joel (1787-1867), m 1820, Margery Canan (1797-1876), moved to Franklin County, Ohio, 1835.
  1. Elizabeth (1821), m ———— Rumsey, d, Dublin, O.
    1. Anna, m Sells.
        Three sons and three daughters.
    2. James, m ————.
  2. John (1824), m Emily ————, Dublin, O.
    1. Mary, m Williams.
        Three sons and two daughters.
    2. Margery, m ———— Wren.
        Two sons and one daughter.
    3. Joan, d
    4. Kate, d
    5. Clara, d
    6. James.
  3. Anna Mary (1828-57), m 1853, Joseph Carroll.
  4. James C. (1830), a mute.
  5. Henry C. (1833), m 1858, Mary E. Kling, Elmwood, Ohio.
    1. Frank, d
    2. Anna Mary.
    3. Williard, m ————.

4. Kate E., m Hall.
    Son and daughter.
5. Harry.
IV. Benjamin (1793 1863), m Mary Caracker (1791 1868).
    Known as the mathematician.
  1. Nicholas (1822 97), m 1844, Anna Cross (1825
    91), known as auctioneer and politician. Alex-
    andria.
    1. Silas W., first wife, Annsavilla Isenberg, d 1885,
      of Enoch of Enoch, Denver, Col.
      Mary Etta, m 1883, Mortimer M. Jones, Den-
      ver, Col.
      Earl S., d
      Adda J., m 1891, Ralph C. Kerr, Mercer.
      Roxanna, m 1889, James E. Nolan, Denver.
      Colorado.
      Edna M., Madelon, Edward W., Earl P.
      Vertie I., d
      Lula Eldora, m 1895, Bert C. Reeves, Denver,
      Colorado.
      Cora M.
      Emma L.
    Second wife, Maria M. Fulk, d 1900.
    2. Mary Etta, m Dr. D. P. Stewart, Sharon.
      Dr. Fred A
      Mary E., m H. E. Paul, Homestead.
      Ella R., m G. A. Baird, Chicago.
    3. Jacob L., m Nettie Taylor, Enid, O. T.
      Clara B., d
      Edna A., m ———— Shoemaker.
      Hollis N. A., Denver, Col.
    4. Wheeler B., m 1895, Ella McGowan, D. D. S.,
      Sharon.
      Anna L., Mary E., Jennie M., Helen C.

5. Benjamin F., first wife, Susan Malseed, d, Alex-
    andria.
    Second wife, Annie Householder.
    Charles F., Sidney D., Oscar L., Wheeler G.

2. William (1823-79), first wife, 1846, Dorothy Isen-
    berg, d 1848, of Joseph of Enoch.

    1. Drucilla, d
        Second wife, 1855, Margaret Shaffer, (1830-99).

    2. Howard R., m 1881, Mary E. Downing, Isett,
        Blair County.
        William E., Ruth, Bessie S., Walter D., Harry
        S., Frederick R

    3. Elsie M., m 1879, James Kelley, Altoona.

    4. Kate, m 1883, John A. Keller, Altoona.
        Calvin R., Ralph K., Franklin P., Mary E.

    5. Harry S., m 1883, Alice Tennis, Altoona.
        Three children, all d.

    6. Alice (1859-99).

3. Daniel, d at 21.

4. Eve, d, maiden lady, Shafersville.

5. Mary, d 1899, m ——— Keller, Shafersville.

    1. Laura, m ——— Garner.

    2. Gemmil.

    3. Hollis.

    4. Kate.

    5. Etta, m ——— Hommer.

V. William (1798-1877, m Elizabeth Roseborough (1806-
        83). Had sixteen children, twelve of whom
        grew to manhood.

    1. Benjamin, d 1897, m 1849, Anna Mary Isenberg of
        Enoch of Enoch.

        1. Sarah, m William E. Henney, Colerain Forge.

        2. Martha L., d, m David L. Isenberg, d, of William
            of Daniel of Enoch, Alexandria.
            See under same for children.

3. W. Hewitt, m Kate Smith, daughter of Margaret Isenberg, of Daniel of Enoch, Huntingdon. Emory N., Alfred P., Martin U., Benjamin F., Milton H., Iva B., John W, N., James S. Paul Z., Carl W., Anna R., Mary M., Ella I.

4. Iva Esther.

5. John V., m Minnie Young, Huntingdon.
Clair W. and William Y.

6. Susan N., m W. Walter Coffman, Huntingdon.
Geary, Louella G., Anna J., Hilda V.,Julia E., Mary E.

7. Roberta, m Orval E. Henney, Huntingdon.
Warrel F., William I., Frederick R.

8. Mary H., m Frank Cozzen, Arch Springs, Blair County.
Four other children died young.

2. Rebecca (1827-59), m 1846, John Forest.

1. Ellen, m James Smith, Tyrone.
Eight children.

2. Francis, m John Smith, Pittsburg.
Six children.

3. Hannah, Alexandria.

4. Samuel (1857-85).

3. Rosannah, maiden lady, Alexandria.

4. Maria, m 1859, John Shultzaberger, Huntingdon.

1. Rose E., m 1885, George Mosser, Huntingdon.
Anna, John, Leroy, Ida, Robert.

5. John, m 1858, Minerva Shively, died in War of the Rebellion, 1865.

1. Elmer, m Iva Flemming, Alexandria.
Four daughters.

2. Harry, m Mary Hashberger, Alexandria.
Five children.

6. William, d at 14.

7. Sarah, m 1854, Jacob Isenberg of Enoch of Enoch, Alexandria.

For children see under the same.

8. Kieffer (1841–97), m 1864, Lucy Dunlap, d 1899, Hood River, Oregon.

    1. Lewis, m Cora Fuller, Hood River, Oregon.

        Victor.

9. Miles Peter (1843), m 1866, Tillie Jones (1846), Hood River, Oregon.

    1. Lydia E., m Simon W. Arnold.

        Flora S. and Clyde H.

    2. Anna E.

    3. Alfred.

    4. F. Howard.

    5. Marshall H.

    6. Walter A.

    7. Ellie.

    8. Elmer W.

    9. Pearl T.

   10. Lena L.

10. Susan, m 1867, William Peterson, d 1873.

    1. Elizabeth, m Wilson Lewis, Tyrone.

        Two children.

11. Louisa, m 1872, John Koser, Alexandria.

    1. Rebecca, m William Corbin, Huntingdon.

    2. Maud.

    3. Gilbert S.

    4. John H.

    5. Charles H.

12. Marshall, m 1874, Clara Cozzen, Arch Springs.

      Lewis K., Rose J., Alfred, Samuel, Lizzie.

VI. Eve, d. m Andrew Mattern, d

        Catharine, John, Mary, Nicholas, George

        Elizabeth, m Jacob Nicely, Joel, William

Abraham. All are dead except three, but which they are, cannot state.

VII. Ann Margaret, d, m 1824, John Piper, d.

1. Anna Mary, d, m William Kemp, d
    1. Alban M., d
    2. John R., Pittsburg.
    3. Joseph M. Altoona.
    4. William M., d
    5. Mary F.
2. John H., d
3. Julia Ann, m Joseph Piper of Philip, Alexandria.
    1. Emory G., Tyrone.
    2. George B., Tyrone.
    3. John H., Altoona.
    4. Alban, Altoona.
    5. Anna.
    6. Edwin.
4. Peter, m 1863, Isabel Isenberg.
        For children see under Daniel of Enoch.
5. William T., single, Alexandria.
6. Nicholas, m Susan C. Hoffman.
        For children see under Anna Mary Hoffman of Enoch.

VIII. Mary Salome, m Samuel Stewart, Mo.

1. David, Cal.
2. James, d
3. William, Mo.
4. Benjamin, Wash.
5. Elizabeth, m Jacob Flood, Mo
6. Ann, m a Smith, d, Mo.

Peter Isenberg's Descendants.

I. Johnathan (1801-72), m 1826, Elizabeth Gahagan (1807-
    97). Watchman, Altoona.

1. John Perry (1827-63) (Shorty John), m 1854, Re-
    becca Bartow.
    1. William G. (1855-56).
    2. Rolandus Alban (1856), m 1878, Martha C. Eb-
        right. Machinist, Altoona.
        Mary Ann.
        John Barkley.
        Leila May.
    3. Plesent Elizabeth (1858), m 1881, William Lane,
        Allegheny.
        Jerry, d, Emma, Ella May, d, Charles, d,
        William, Sadie, Nellie.
    4. John Perry (1859), m 1884, Kate Coulter, Con-
        ductor, Altoona.
        Maud Ethel, John William d, Cloy Edna,
        Ralph Elton, Chester Allen, d
    5. Mary Jane (1863), m 1884, James Shultzaberger,
        Bellwood, boiler maker.
        Gertie May, Jesse Allen, Annie E., d, Rebec-
        ca F., d, James C.
2. Annalisa (1829-33).
3. Margaret Jane (1831-33).
4. James G. (1834-89), m Catharine Morgan, d, killed
    by engine at Harrisburg. Engineer.
    1. Missouri Ann (1856-1900), m 1877, Joseph Gar-
        verich (1851-97), Baltimore, Md.
    2. Alonzo Jonathan (1858), m 1884, Carrie Webber.
        Hotel proprietor, Toledo, O.
        Harry Wayne.

Alonza Jonathan, Jr.

Bessie Irene.

3. Alfred James (1861), m 1895, Annie E. Foster.
Engineer, Delphos, O.

4. Mary Margaret (1865), m 1886, William Sum-
mers, Baltimore, Md.

Charles W.

Willie.

Ethel May, d

5. Ida May (1868), first husband, Deatrick.

Maud Lenora.

Second husband, 1895, William Brown, d,
Baltimore.

5. Mary Ann (1839-41).

6. Plesent Elizabeth(1847), m John Columbus, Story, O.
Two children.

II. Philip (1803-86), moved to Ohio, Fredericktown, Knox
County, 1835, m 1838, Sarah L. Burkholder
(1814-88).

1. Jacob D. (1840-69) Co. A 20 Reg. O. V., 1861-64,
m 1865, Louisa J. Murphy.

1. John L. (1866), m 1892, Cora McConnell, Caldwell, Idaho.

Fredda.

2. Jacob G., (1869-1888).

2. Elizabeth (1843), m 1874, Daniel M. Follin, Bangorville, O.

1. Emma (1875), m 1897, Murray Agnew, Fredericktown, O.

Henry.

2. Mary.

3. Earnest.

3. Catharine (1845-79).

4. George (1845-52).

5. Margaret (1849), m 1879, Amariah C. Huntsman, Darlington, O.
   Mary.

6. Leroy (1852), unmarried, Bangorville, O.

7. Lorain (1852), m 1882, Narcissa E. Zimmerman. Physician, Shreve, O.
   Kitty and Edna M., d, Zella.

III. Mordecai (1806-69), m 1828, Elizabeth Heckendorn. Lived near Alexandria on farm now owned by Elwood M. Isenberg.

1. Mary Ann. d 1875. m A. B. Flood, Tyrone.
   1. Myra, Huntingdon.
   2. Elmer G., Detroit, Mich.
   3. Carrie A., m W. F. Raymann, Pueblo, Col.
   4. Frank W., Cumberland, Md.
   5. H. Miller.
   6. Jean N., d 1889.
   7. Warren A., d 1892.

2. Sallie Ann, m 1862, Samuel Sprankie, Tyrone.
   1. Bessie C., m Harry Bell.
   2. Harry C., m Mary Fleck.
   3. Emma A., m Wm. McCormick.
      Esther and Robert.
   4. Frank I., m Florence Snook.
      Virginia, Clifford, Alma.
   5. Howard S., m Carrie Smith.
      Chester.
   6. H. Jean, m Charles Eyer.
   7. Viola Mary.
   8. J. Carl.

3. David Allen (1837-66), m 1864, Virginia Buckingham, M. E. minister.
   Mamie Allen 1866, married 1863, J. C. Field, Brooklyn, New York.
   Addie Virginia.

4. Hannah, maiden lady, Tyrone.
5. Margaret E., m Longwell, Tower Hill, Ill.
      E. Plummer, Cloyd, Carlton, Bessie.
6. Nicholas Smouse, m ———, Company C, 125th
      Reg. Pa. Vols., Ventura, Cal.
      Bertha, Mabel, Trevor.
7. Peter Sprankle, m ———, Bellwood.
      Wm. Walter, Alvin, David, John, Arthur.

IV. David, m Agnes Mooney, both d, lived in Port Royal.
1. Margaret, d, m ———,
      Two sons, two daughters, one d
2. Elizabeth, m ———.
3. Philip, d, m ———.
      Two sons, one d, three daughters.
4. Charlotte, m ———, Perry County.
      Five daughters, one d
5. Mordecai M., m 1861, Elmira J. Casner, Mifflintown,
      Pa.
  1. Wm. C., m Jane Varns.
      Seven children, one d.
  2. Ellen A., m W. R. Dalton
      Three children.
  3. David, d.
  4. Annie E., m J. W. Hile.
      Three children, one d.
  5. James B., m Emma B. Cox.
  6. Minnie M., m T. A. Long.
      Three children, one d.
  7. Emma B., m Stewart Horning.
      Two children, one d.
  8. John H., m Bertha Dunn.
      One child.
  9. Daniel A.
  10. Gertrude A.

6. Salome, maiden lady.
7. Joel, d, m.
        Son and daughter, d.
8. Amos, d, m.
        Three sons and five daughters, all d but daughter.
9. Hossannah, d.
10. Hannah M., m ————, Harrisburg.
11. William, m ————, Perry County.
        Three sons, two d, and two daughters.
12. Johnathan, d.
V. Hannah, died young.

All orders for this book will be filled by E. S. Burket, Martinsburg, Pa.

www.ingramcontent.com/pod-product-compliance
Lightning Source LLC
Chambersburg PA
CBHW050537280326
41933CB00011B/1618